BULLIED
From Terror to
TRIUMPH

My Survival Story
TENSIE J. TAYLOR

BULLIED FROM TERROR TO TRIUMPH, MY SURVIVAL STORY

Published by Lee's Press and Publishing Company
2618 Battleground Ave
STE A #233
Greensboro, NC 27408

This document is published by Lee's Press and Publishing Company
located in the United States of America. It is protected by the United
States Copyright Act, all applicable state laws and international
copyright laws. The information in this document is accurate to the
best of the ability of the author at the time of writing. The content of
this document is subject to change without notice.

ISBN-13: 978-0692622193 *Paperback*
ISBN-10: 0692622195

Library of Congress Cataloging-in-Publication Data

CONTENTS

Contents

Foreword

Bullying is one of the greatest threats to the social, emotional, and psychological well-being of children, with the potential to affect them well into adulthood. Many of the youth and adults I see in my practice have experienced some form of bullying that has impacted their self-esteem. In some cases, acts of bullying have contributed to feelings of depression and anxiety which persists into adulthood. There is a need for those who have overcome the lethal effects of bullying to share their stories to help to empower those who feel disempowered by those who bully.

Tensie J. Taylor has done just that in her new hallmark book entitled, "BULLIED From Terror to Triumph, My Survival Story." Ms. Taylor provides readers with the opportunity to experience the pain she endured during her early school years. But most importantly, readers will learn how to overcome the negative effects of bullying. In this book, Ms. Taylor shares her story of triumph, and encourages those who are being bullied to suffer in silence no more. I highly recommend everyone to read "BULLIED From Terror to Triumph, My Survival Story," especially those who have a history of being bullied. This prolific autobiography should be required reading for all those who bully.

Thank you Ms. Tensie J. Taylor for your transparency and bravery. Your testimony will help and inspire the masses. You are a modern day heroine.

Gloria Morrow, Ph.D.
Licensed Clinical Psychologist
GM Psychological Services, Inc.

Preface

The purpose of this book is to share my story about the physical, verbal, and emotional bullying I experienced at school from kindergarten through twelfth grade. I am vulnerable and transparent with my story in hopes of raising further awareness about bullying and providing suggestions and recommendations on how I survived this treatment. It is **not** my intention to be malicious by telling the names of the people who bullied me in school, and for this reason, all students' names that are in *italics* are pseudo names. However, the teachers' names who are listed in this book were my real teachers in school, and their names have not been changed because they were positive influences in my life.

Thank you to my Dr. Gloria Morrow for writing the foreword to this book and for being so supportive and inspirational to me. As a psychologist, she understands why people behave in a particular manner and states the importance of healing, redemption, and forgiveness.

To my family, friends, teachers, and mentors, thank you for helping to mold me into the person I am today. It is because of you that I continued to stay motivated and encouraged.

To those who are bullied, I hope my story gives you hope and courage to go on in spite of life's challenges and to ignore the negativity from others. I pray that our world will become more loving and caring and that we start to show more kindness and gentleness to one another. God bless.

Tensie J. Taylor, M.Ed.

Chapter 1

August 25, 1992

"Jannniinneeeeee, time to wake up. It's the first day of school!" I remember the day as if it were yesterday. I eagerly woke up to the sing-song voice of my mother and the beautiful sunrays peeking through my bedroom window. The birds were chirping loudly and singing so mellifluously that they, too, were excited for my big day. As Mom lightly tapped me on my shoulder and sweetly told me to get up, it was evident she shared in my enthusiasm because it was my official first day of kindergarten.

I immediately hopped out of bed and began getting ready for school. I picked out my outfit the night before: a simple, yet elegant white blouse, a knee-length pink skirt with ruffles at the bottom, white laced socks, and pink shoes called jellies. While I was getting dressed, the wonderful aroma of delicious southern food permeated throughout the house. I instantly knew it was Dad making one of his famous breakfasts. I finished getting ready and hurriedly ran to the kitchen table.

"Good Morning Daddy!" I exclaimed, as I sat down eagerly waiting for him to serve me.

"Good Morning Janine. Are you ready for your first day of kindergarten?"

"Yes sir, I am ready!" I replied, as I put a big spoonful of grits in my mouth. As much as I wanted to enjoy the delicious eggs, grits, sausage, and bacon that

Dad made, I was too excited to eat and ended up eating only a handful of food.

I could not believe the time had finally arrived; I was starting school. Numerous thoughts crossed my mind as I pondered about the friends I would make, the games I would play, the coursework I would learn, and the number of students in my class. Then my inquisitive nature kicked in. Would my teacher be friendly? Would I enjoy the food at lunch? Would I have fun sliding down the slide on the playground? Would I still be the smallest person in the room? Simply put, I was happy!

After breakfast, Mom braided my hair to make sure I looked nice for school. I had long, thick hair that she braided into four pigtails. To put the finishing touches on my hairstyle, she tied a beautiful pink bow on each braid.

"There!" she said. "You look adorable."

I quickly ran to the mirror to see how I looked, and Mom was right; I did look cute. I gave her a huge hug as she wished me a wonderful first day of school and handed me my red lunch box. After she helped me put on my Barbie book bag, I exclaimed, "Bye Mom!" as I feverishly waved to her like Forrest did when he saw Lieutenant Dan on the boat in the movie *Forrest Gump*.

"Bye Pooh Cake. Have a great day!" she responded, as I happily skipped outside to the car where Dad was waiting to take me to St. Paul's Daycare Center.

The bus did not pass by my parents' house to take me to Louisburg Elementary School, so Dad dropped me off at the daycare to catch the bus there. I began humming to myself and the more I thought about school, the more excited I became. I could not wait to arrive at the daycare so I could finally get to school!

I graduated from St. Paul's Daycare Center at the age of four. I learned a plethora of information from my teachers, and they prepared me for my elementary education. Mrs. Privette and her staff taught me my ABCs, numbers, songs, and dances. I knew how to say my grace before each meal, and all of Mrs. Privette's babies—as she liked to call us—were well behaved.

Mrs. Privette was such a warm, caring, and loving woman, but she demanded respect and manners from her babies. This was easy for me to abide by because my parents taught me manners and respect at home. If I did not behave, I faced the consequences both at school and at home. I was also confident in my academic abilities and knew I was prepared for kindergarten because St. Paul's Daycare Center provided an excellent educational foundation.

After what seemed like an eternity, Dad and I pulled up to the daycare center. He walked me inside, said a hearty "Good morning" to all the staff, parents and kids, signed me in, gave me a hug and kiss on the cheek, and wished me a terrific first day of school. I went into the room for school children ages five to ten years old and eagerly waited until my bus arrived.

"The bus is here," said Ms. Josephine. Ms. Josephine was one of the daycare staff members. She was an older lady who had worked many years at the daycare center. She was very sweet, kind, and gentle, and the students loved her dearly.

I grabbed my pink Barbie book bag, waved goodbye to the daycare personnel, and with a huge smile on my face, ran outside to board school bus 144.

"Good morning!" I said excitedly to the bus driver Mr. Edwards. He mumbled something back to me, and I took my seat in the front of the bus. Mr. Edwards was an older, white gentleman who wore a dark blue uniform. He did not say much to any of us, and he walked as slowly as he drove. Even as a child, I was observant and knew the speed limit on the bus was 45 mph, but sometimes I thought I was the backseat passenger in *Driving Miss Daisy* because of how slowly Mr. Edwards drove. I guess he was being extra cautious. Nonetheless, we always got to school safely, and that was a blessing.

The daycare was close to Louisburg Elementary School, and the ride to school was quick. Mr. Edwards pulled up to the bus parking lot, and we were the first bus to arrive. We sat and waited for a few minutes as other buses started to arrive. After what seemed like an eternity, Mr. Edwards opened the bus door, and the students rushed off. I could hardly wait to get to class and learn.

I stepped off of bus number 144 and proceeded to walk to class. After a few steps, my gait came to an immediate and unexpected halt as someone jerked my book bag from behind. I turned around and saw a tall, black, female student much bigger than me glaring down at my face. She viciously snatched my pink, Barbie book bag off my back, unzipped it, and threw all my belongings on the ground. As I watched my crayons, Barbie coloring book, paper, pencil holder, pens, markers, and journal all tumble to the ground, I profusely blinked my eyes thinking that I must be dreaming. I saw my pink Barbie book bag dangling in her hands, and my thoughts were interrupted when I heard her tauntingly yell at me,

"Hey! Pick it up! You better not try nothin' neither!"

By this time, a crowd of students had gathered around me, and I was certain at least one person would come to my rescue and help me. To my surprise, no one did. Instead, the students pointed and laughed at me, which gave the bully more fuel to make a mockery of me. With tears in my eyes, I slowly knelt down on the hot, hard, asphalt (getting my pink skirt dirty), picked up my belongings the bully threw on the ground, and began placing the items back inside my pink Barbie bag.

I kept hoping and wishing that someone would lend a hand and help me off the ground and gather my belongings; this never happened. Choking back the tears and trying to drown out the students' taunts and jeers, I got up off the ground, dusted my skirt off, put my book bag back on, and headed towards my class. August 25, 1992—at the tender age of five—marked the first day of being bullied for the next thirteen years of my life.

The happiness and vivacity I felt when I woke up for school that morning had dissipated. I walked into Mrs. May's classroom with my head held low and took my seat. I did not want to learn; I did not want to make a new friend; I did not want to go outside and play. All I wanted to do was go home, get in my bed, hide under the covers, hold my stuffed animal, and cry. My first day of school was a blur, literally and figuratively. My vision was blurred from continually blinking back the tears, and it was blurred because I do not recollect much of what I learned that day. I was more focused on keeping my eyes peeled and ears open to make sure I avoided the bully because I did not want to cross paths with her again. I did not even know her, but I was already afraid of her. On that first day, I was not sure of her name, but as the torment continued for the next three years, she later became one of the meanest students who bullied me.

I kept quiet in class and for the most part, stayed to myself, never interacting with fellow classmates at lunch or recess. The little I do remember on that day was how extremely nice and caring my teacher, Mrs. May, was. I liked her because she had such a motherly quality and was so warm and friendly. Even in spite of my teacher's warmness, the only thing that continued flooding my mind was my desire to go home. I felt so powerless, voiceless, helpless, and hopeless. I was already a shy, little girl, and this incident contributed more to my timidity. I was afraid to ride the school bus that afternoon, thinking the bully would be on it again. I breathed a refreshing sigh of relief when I saw the last person board and thankfully, it was not her.

That evening during our family dinner, my parents asked,

"How was your first day of school?"

I looked down at my plate and began spreading butter beans around with my fork. I gave a generic answer, tried to put on a façade as if everything were okay and softly responded,

"It was nice. I met my classmates and I really like my teacher Mrs. May."

It worked. Mom and Dad never suspected that anything went wrong that day, but I knew August 25, 1992 would forever be etched in my mind.

Chapter 2

The Early Years

I was born in Henderson, North Carolina at Maria Parham Hospital on August 19, 1987 at 8:30 a.m. to Robert and Levonia Taylor. Mom jokes that I came out the womb hollering and screaming, and at that moment, she knew I had excellent lungs and would be loquacious; she was right. My brother Jemonde and sister Kelise, made their entry into the world a little more quietly than I did. I presume I wanted the world to know I had arrived, and I did. Mom named me after my aunt, her sister, Tensie Dale. Even though Tensie is my first name, I was called by my middle name Janine, at home.

I was raised in a small city named Louisburg, which is approximately thirty miles north of the capital of North Carolina, Raleigh. This is my hometown, and I am proud to have been raised there. I was born into a middle class family, where my parents were both educators. Dad taught English, African-American Literature, and French on both the high school and collegiate level for 48 years, and Mom was a Librarian and taught at elementary, middle, and high schools in North Carolina for 38 years. Because my parents are so educated, I know my English, African-American history, and library skills pretty well. If someone were to ask me to diagram a sentence, to give the definition of *triskaidekaphobia*, to explain the significant contributions of Crispus Attucks, or to provide an overview of the

Dewey Decimal System, I could expound on each of these topics effortlessly.

Even up until this day, Dad still speaks French fluently. The only French I know is *oui* and *si'l vous plait*. There were many times while growing up that people used the pronoun *we* to describe something that did not turn out favorably and tried to include me in the mix. My response was always the same:

"We? We? When did you start speaking French? There is no *we* messed up. It is *you* who messed up."

That is all the French I know. Dad tried to teach me this romance language when I was a kid. He bought me books, cassette tapes, and showed me French lessons he taught his students. Instead of learning French, I was more interested in playing with my Barbie car, learning miniature golf, coloring in my Barbie book, or pondering why I was the smallest person everywhere I went. I regret never learning this language, despite Dad's efforts in trying to teach me.

I was blessed to have a beautiful childhood. I had two parents, who loved me dearly, a brother Jemonde who was my protector and best friend, and a sister Kelise who played Barbie dolls with me. I lived in a nice house, had my own bed, had plenty of toys to play with, a piano to "tickle the ivories" on, a library to read books, and was constantly showered with love and praise. I was tremendously proud of my parents because they came from such humble beginnings and grew up extremely poor. As Dad jokes, "I wasn't poor, I was po.'"

Mom was a sharecropper and worked from sunup to sundown on the farm and lived in a shack with her parents and three siblings as a child. Dad lived in a house with a special kind of running water.

"I had to run down to the well, fetch the water, and run back." Dad chuckled as he told the story. "This was the running water we had in my house." He jokes about this now, but back then, it was a difficult time for his family.

Growing up, my parents shared these stories with my siblings and me to tell us how far they had come and to instill in us that anything could be accomplished with hard work and determination. I listened to their stories in amazement because they had been through so much and faced numerous struggles, and yet, they were still in jovial spirits, enjoyed life, and appreciated their blessings while being a blessing to others. The one ideal they constantly instilled in me was education. Dad always said that education would open numerous doors of opportunity. Education was taken very seriously in my parents' home, and they expected nothing but excellence from us. Even if we did not get an A or B, as long as we tried our best, was all they required.

My parents taught me manners. I was to never answer an adult by saying 'What?' 'Huh?' 'What you say?' unless I wanted to be toothless for the rest of my life. Mom did not play that, and because I knew not to cross her, I am blessed to have all my pearly, white teeth today. Mom and Dad taught me to say "Yes Ma'am, no sir, please, thank you, excuse me, and pardon me." I was to never call an adult by his/her first name. I addressed him/her as Mr., Mrs., or Dr. to show respect. These are characteristics I still use today, which have contributed to my advancement in life.

Mom was a stickler for showing appreciation and gratitude. She instilled in me that when someone does something nice for a person, such as give a birthday gift, a graduation gift, or any type of gift, one must show appreciation by writing a thank you note.

I grew up in the 90s during the generation where writing emails or sending text messages were practically non-existent. Even if it had been popular, Mom would not have allowed me to do it because she said that sending a handwritten thank you letter was more meaningful. At four years old, I began writing thank you letters. My mother first crafted these letters for me and then showed me how to use my own words and vocabulary to express my gratitude. At four years old, writing a thank you letter was the farthest thing from my mind. I wanted to play with my Barbie dolls or go outside and swing on the swing set, but I couldn't, because the thing that stood in my way was writing a thank you letter.

I have always been a small and creative person. Even at 28 years old at the time of this book's publication, I am still very small and creative. I remember watching episodes of *Sanford and Son*, and Fred got out of doing something for Lamont by pretending he had arthritis. I had no earthly idea what arthritis was, but I knew that Fred would cripple his fingers and say he could not perform a task because of this ailment.

One day, when I desperately wanted to go outside and play on the swing set, I told Mom that I wished I could write a thank you letter, but my arthritis would not allow me to do so. Trying to look as pathetic and pitiful as I could, I dropped my pen and crippled my hands just as Fred had done on *Sanford and Son*. With my stellar acting skills, I knew I would be outside playing on the swing set in no time. Mom simply smiled, took off her flip flop, looked down at me and said,

"Either you write this thank you note or you will feel this flip flop against your hind part."

Immediately, Jesus performed one of His miracles, and my arthritis instantly subsided! I was familiar with Jesus' miraculous stories from Bible study, but I had no idea He could perform them so quickly. Miraculously, my arthritis healed, and I began writing my thank you letter. That flip flop cured my arthritis, and oh how powerful this object was. Who knew that something so small could cure a four year old's arthritis? To this day, I have never had another bout with arthritis, especially when I have to write a thank you note.

I thank Mom so much for showing and teaching me the importance of thank you notes, even if she did have to take off her flip flop and threaten me. My thank you letters have touched the hearts of many and have afforded me numerous opportunities throughout life. Showing appreciation to someone is one of the best things a person can do. A person does not always have to give a lavish or expensive gift to show someone that (s)he cares, but something as simple as saying *thank you* and expressing it in words can mean the world.

Being from a family that focused heavily on values and respect, I was naïve and assumed that every person in each household was raised this way. Mom and Dad told me to follow the Golden Rule: *Do unto others as you would have them do unto you.* I followed this rule by treating people respectfully, speaking to everyone I met and showing genuine compassion towards people. Yet, I quickly learned that everyone was not raised like me. As my school days continued, students would show me who they really were by their actions and words.

Chapter 3

The Taunting and Teasing Begin

There were many students who were cruel to me, said hurtful remarks about me, wished me failure at school, made fun of my parents' car, and taunted me because I did not wear name-brand clothes or shoes. While I was in elementary school, I never wore one outfit that was name-brand nor were my shoes name-brand. At the time, my parents could not afford to buy me these things, and they were also teaching me that there were more to clothes than a name.

Before each school year started, my parents took me school clothes shopping at Wal-Mart or Family Dollar because that is all they could afford on their teacher's salary while raising three kids. Although we shopped at these places, my parents were very smart and had their priorities in order. I may not have worn Nike or Adidas shoes, but my parents paid their mortgage and monthly bills on time. I learned the value of a dollar and saw firsthand that my parents invested their money on important items, and not on trivial material things, such as a $90 shirt or $300 shoes.

Mom liked buying me shoes that had velcro, and I thought these shoes were cool because of the sound it made. I pulled apart the velcro many times at home until I annoyed practically everyone in the house. To me, velcro was stylish, and I expected the students at school to compliment me on my shoes. I could not have been more wrong in my life.

After the initial first day of bullying, my days of feeling safe at the front of the bus were over. The reason I felt safe at the front was because I was close to the bus driver, and I doubted that a student would bully me next to an adult. One morning as I boarded the bus, I noticed that Mr. Edwards had given us assigned seats by last name. Because my last name began with a 'T,' I sat at the back of the school bus. My main bully *Sandy*, the one who began terrorizing me on that dreadful day of August 25, 1992, last name began with an 'M,' and she sat in front of me. While riding to school, I looked straight ahead, but *Sandy* deliberately turned around and taunted me. I tried to avoid looking at her, but each time, she maliciously said,

"Who you think you looking at? Stop looking at me with yo' ugly self!"

I tried to ignore *Sandy* as best as I could.

One morning, Mr. Edwards thought he would be fair and let the back of the bus get off first. This was music to my ears because it meant I could get off the bus before *Sandy* did and quickly run to class. Normally, I was unable to do this when Mr. Edwards let the front of the bus get off first because *Sandy* got off before me and waited for me, just to terrorize me.

I was too focused on getting off the bus before *Sandy* that when I walked past her on the bus, I did not notice she had stuck her foot out to trip me. I might have fallen flat on my face if I had not fallen into the person in front of me who was exiting the bus. The students were in an uproar of laughter, and the person in front of me angrily pushed me off and yelled,

"Get off me!"

This only made my classmates laugh louder, and I choked back the tears and hurriedly got off the bus.

Trying so desperately not to cry, I ran to my first grade class, and my teacher's name was Mrs. Harrison. Much like my kindergarten teacher Mrs. May, Mrs. Harrison was a lovely woman and an awesome teacher. I enjoyed her teaching style, and she helped me get out of my shy shell. She worked diligently with me and on one occasion when I received my report card, she wrote that I was blossoming nicely in class. To further encourage my early leadership skills, Mrs. Harrison made me the class line leader. I was so proud and happy to be the line leader, and I wanted to make sure I looked extra nice on the days I was to lead the line.

One particular week as line leader, I decided to wear my velcro shoes with one of my favorite outfits: cardinal-colored corduroy shorts and a white Louisburg Elementary School Field Day shirt. I knew I was stylish and would receive compliments on my outfit that day. I was wrong.

That afternoon during recess, several students came up and began taunting me,

"You have on some ugly shoes. You got on skips."

Skips was a term used to describe non name-brand shoes. These students wore Nike's, Adidas', Jordan's, and I had on my special non name-brand shoes with velcro. When they started making fun of my shoes, I became extremely embarrassed and ashamed of the shoes I was once so proud of. I began to get upset with my parents and secretly blamed them for not buying me name-brand shoes or clothes. I believed that if I had name-brand clothing, I would get picked on less.

Even though I did not get to wear name-brand clothes, Mom always made sure I dressed neatly and nicely. She liked matching colors, and one outfit I wore to school consisted of a white shirt with yellow lions with bright yellow pants to match. The school year had worn on, and now it was late fall. I wore a coat to school, and when I took my coat off, a student said,

"You look like Big Bird with all that yallo' on."

I already felt self-conscious about my clothes and while I was in my thoughts, two things came to mind: One, this student had the nerve to pick on my clothes when she couldn't even properly pronounce the word *yellow*. Two, it was my own black race who picked on me the most.

As my time at Louisburg Elementary School went on, I continued to face verbal forms of bullying, especially during recess. When most kids could not wait to go outside for recess, I was the exact opposite because this is where I was bullied heavily. Teachers could not be everywhere, and students knew this. Bullies often gathered in circles around me and poked fun of my size, intellect, height, hair, nose, forehead, complexion, eyes, shoes, and clothes. Girls sometimes pulled my hair and said,

"You think you all dat cuz you light-skinned."

Never once did I think I was better than anyone because of the complexion of my skin nor did these words ever come out of my mouth.

Out of the many times I was bullied in elementary school, there was only one time I stood up for myself. I was ten years old and a fifth grade student in Mr. McLaughlin's class. Mr. McLaughlin stepped out of the classroom for a moment to make a few extra copies of an assignment. As soon as he left, *Casey*, a student in my class who constantly picked on my clothes, said,

"Hey, who in here has on skips?"

My classmates looked around the room and *Casey* continued,

"Tensie does! Tensie does!"

Casey was a brown skin, black female who was so developed that she looked more like an adult than a fifth grader. She came to school with dirty clothes and had poor dental hygiene. *Casey* pointed at my shoes, and the whole class erupted in laughter. I was mortified and began to turn red. I was focusing on my schoolwork, not bothering anyone, and yet again, the attention was turned on me. By this time, I had had enough and was fed up with people picking on me while I sat quietly, not defending myself. Before I knew it, I turned around to *Casey* and said,

"*Casey*, I'd rather wear skips than come to school stinky like you! At least I live in a nice, brick, house and don't live in an ugly trailer like you. You come to school wearing dirty clothes so, you're one to talk!"

At that moment, the laughter stopped and my classmates said "Oooooo" and some began laughing at her. *Casey* was so upset and had tears in her eyes that as soon as Mr. McLaughlin came back to the classroom, she asked to go to the office to call her Mom. She was so upset and hurt by my words that her Mom came to school and picked her up. I did not feel any shame for what I said. Since third grade, she had teased and taunted me, pushed me, made fun of my clothes, and yelled at me, and I said nothing. However, I finally stood up for myself by making one comment, a true comment, and she goes running out the classroom crying to her mommy.

Later that night, *Casey's* Mom called my Mom to say how badly I hurt her feelings. Mom told *Casey's* Mom that I did not have to apologize to her because she had been picking on me for the past two years. A small sense of confidence filled me, and I felt proud of myself. After being bullied for five years at school, I had finally stood up for myself, and the reaction was priceless. Needless to say, *Casey* never had anything else to say to me for the rest of the year, but her bullying stopped only temporarily.

Chapter 4

Transferring to a New School

The bullying continued long after my first day of school in 1992 at Louisburg Elementary School. *Sandy* kept making fun of me and still physically and verbally abused me. I was so afraid at school that I feared walking down the hallway alone to go to the bathroom or riding the bus with *Sandy*. There were several students who made fun of me, but *Sandy* terrorized me, and enjoyed getting satisfaction in knowing I was terribly afraid of her.

After spending three years at Louisburg Elementary School, I was thrilled when Mom told me she was applying for a Librarian position at Laurel Mill Elementary School. I was excited more so for me because if she received this position, I could transfer to a new school and would no longer fear being verbally and physically bullied at Louisburg Elementary School.

Mom received the news that she had gotten the position as Librarian at Laurel Mill Elementary School. I was absolutely ecstatic because I was confident that with my Mom at school, the bullying would decrease. I was very optimistic that having her at school would make my life easier. I was ready to leave Louisburg Elementary School and my main bully, *Sandy*, behind. I would miss my teachers and the few friends I had, but I was ready to embark on a new adventure, a new environment, and I was looking forward to what was to come.

My first day of school of my third grade year arrived. I felt so much relief in many areas. I no longer rode the school bus or worried about being tripped or having my belongings snatched off my back. Now, I felt safe riding to school with Mom. It was Mom and me, no bullies, no people to make fun of me, nothing. I felt free.

For my first day of school outfit, I wore a white and pink blouse, a blue and pink striped skirt, black shoes, and my hair in pigtails. I hoped Mom would let me wear my hair loose, but she said I couldn't. On my first day attending Laurel Mill Elementary School, I was so nervous and scared, but my fear slightly subsided when I recognized a familiar face in my class.

Having a familiar face in class made me feel a little more confident. I had successfully gotten through a half day at a new school without anyone making fun of me, and before I knew it, it was time to line up for lunch. When we walked in a single file line to the cafeteria, I stood in line and watched other students in front of me get their lunch to see how the cafeteria system worked. It was different than Louisburg Elementary School's cafeteria system. I did not want to do anything wrong to embarrass myself, so I watched the mannerisms of other students.

The lunch line was very creative and cute and was in the form of a rocket. Students lined up on both sides, picked up a tray, and served themselves through the line. This looked simple enough, and I was confident I could navigate this line successfully. I picked up my tray, placed the items that I wanted on it, paid the cashier, and searched for a familiar face to sit beside. I was unable to find my friend, so I decided to sit at a table with new faces.

One of the new faces was that of a student named *Charles*. I sat down at the table, and he gave me the meanest and coldest look and said,

"Who is you? I neva seen you befoe."

I replied, "Hi, my name is Tensie. I just started going to this school. What's your name?"

He looked me up and down and replied, "Nobody said you could sit here."

His words caught me off guard, and I was shunned. My heart started beating fast and I felt nervously sick. After being at my new school for only a few hours, I already felt out of place and began to question why I could never fit in anywhere I went.

I tried to ignore his comment, picked up my milk carton, and forcefully began to eat my food. My appetite disappeared because of his rude response, but I continued to act as if nothing were wrong and forced my food down, hoping he would not make any more comments. *Charles* detected my body language and could sense I was afraid of him.

From that day forward, I made sure not to sit anywhere close to him and to avoid him at all costs. However, even though I tried to get away from him, he deliberately found his way to me and made sure to sit as close to me as possible. Whenever he was around me, I felt dismal because he mercilessly picked on my clothes, shoes, and forehead. He became so persistent with making fun of me that the more I tried to avoid him, the more he purposefully made sure he was around me. I became so depressed and tired of his behavior that I finally decided to tell my teacher. She pulled him aside and talked to him, which did not do much good. He was a troublemaker and several teachers did not have much control over his behavior in class.

Charles was a male who wore saggy pants to school and oversized t-shirts. He constantly misbehaved in class, was sent to the principal's office numerous times, and was excessively rude and disrespectful to teachers and administrators. He always had a funny smell as if he didn't fully bathe every day, and his clothes looked dirty. He failed a grade previously and education was not a priority of his. He walked around with a limp as if he owned the place, and he was downright mean to me.

One afternoon during lunch while I was at a table eating with my classmates, *Charles* walked up and sat at the end of the table next to me. I viewed him out of my peripheral vision, and I continued looking straight ahead trying not to make eye contact with him. He leaned over and whispered in my ear,

"Tell on me again, and I'll kill you and yo family."

He then got up and walked off, laughing heavily.

My face froze, and I dropped my head and looked down at my plate, hoping my classmates did not suspect anything. *Charles* had scared me terribly, and I was unsure of what to do. During my elementary school days, I did not grow up during the time of school shootings, such as Columbine or Sandy Hook. School shootings were unheard of during my day. *Charles'* words continued to echo in my mind, and I vacillated on what to do. I was terrified and believed that if I told on him, he would harm my family and me.

I decided to tell my teacher, but waited until the school day ended before I confided in her. I was so afraid to approach her, but after I told her, she hugged me and assured me that everything would be alright. After I told her, I walked down to the assistant principal's office and shared with him what *Charles* said to me. The assistant principal took this situation seriously and told me that teachers and administrators would watch me vigilantly. For the rest of the year, teachers watched me at all times, and *Charles* was not to come within a certain amount of feet of me. He got suspended for his threat and after he returned to school, I was extremely afraid of him. There were times when I feigned sickness to avoid going to school because of how scared I was. However, the one thing that made me feel safe was knowing I had a support system.

I do not know what happened to *Charles* after third grade because I never saw him again. I am not sure if he transferred schools or was kicked out of school, nor did I care. I no longer had to see him, be afraid of him, or worry about him threatening my family or me. It was not until years later when I came home from college and drove through downtown Louisburg that I saw *Charles* again. He was hanging on the street corner yelling at someone. Based on how he behaved in school, I was not surprised to see him end up on this path.

Chapter 5

Failing to Fit In

Middle School is an interesting time in a young person's life, especially mine. In middle school, adolescents and teenagers experience puberty, gain a little more responsibility, and have to deal with peer pressure. Thankfully, I had survived elementary school and somehow made it to middle school, despite being bullied. I was optimistic to start a new chapter in my life at a new school.

Before the school year started, I begged Dad to purchase me name-brand clothes in hopes that this would alleviate the bullying. Unfortunately, he did not let me buy a name-brand outfit, but he did purchase me a pair of Nike's. I already felt confident and knew that since I had name-brand shoes, the bullying would hopefully stop.

It was August 1998, my first day of sixth grade at Terrell Lane Middle School, and I remember my first day of school outfit. I wore a red Disneyland shirt that my brother bought me in California, a pair of knee-length white shorts, and my brand new white, blue, and red Nike shoes. I was coordinated from head to toe. I was ready to learn and in the words of James Brown, "I felt good!"

I had Mrs. Hartsfield for Language Arts, and she was an absolutely phenomenal teacher. She was dynamic and taught her students the different parts of speech, how to think critically, and she had us memorize one poem a month. Memorizing a poem a month was my favorite part of her class. To this day, I still know all the poems from her class and can recite them from memory. Poems such as *I Know Something Good about You*, *It Couldn't Be Done*, *Be the Best of Whatever You Are*, and *Think* are still stored in my memory bank. This is how powerful of a teacher she was, and she instilled excellence as well as good mannerisms in her students. I loved her dearly.

I soared and excelled in her class. My grades were 95s and 100s, and being the overachiever I was, I took advantage of all extra credit opportunities. I received 105s and 110s on assignments, and when report card time came around, my average for the class was a 99 or 100. I loved her class, and I had such a penchant for learning. Learning new concepts and analyzing the different parts of a story (climax, foreshadowing, plot, main characters) greatly interested me. However, all of my classmates did not feel this way.

I had ambivalent feelings when Mrs. Hartsfield or my other teachers passed back tests or assignments. I was proud of myself for making excellent grades, but other students in my class were sick of me getting A's. As students typically do, we asked each other what each person made on a test. I tried to look down or away from the conversation, hoping they would not ask me what I received. My looking away did not work because the students always asked what grade I received. I shyly and ashamedly looked at them and said, "I made a

100," or "I made a 103." I never asked what grade they made because I knew if I had, they would think I was trying to rub my grade in their faces. After I told them what I received, the students replied,

"Show off. I can't stand you!"

One time, a fellow classmate remarked,

"You are so selfish. You make all these good grades but won't let nobody cheat off yo paper. You such a goody-two-shoes."

My original feelings of being proud of myself for studying and working hard to make an A, ceased. I was sad and tried to keep myself from crying. I now felt embarrassed for performing well and wondered why students were so mean and picked on me for doing well academically? We were in the same classes, had the same teachers, used the same textbooks, and had the same 24 hours in a day. I chose to study and do well, while they wanted to pass notes during class or go home and play video games. Their lack of studying was their problem, not mine, but I could not understand why they blamed me for not letting them cheat off my paper.

One day while in class, a fellow classmate of mine named *Lauren* snatched my paper off my desk and began copying my answers onto her paper. *Lauren* was almost six feet tall in middle school, and she was notorious for being mean to both students and teachers. Not only did she bully me, but she bullied several other students, too. Yet, she bullied me more because I was much smaller than other students she picked on.

When I tried to take my paper back from *Lauren*, she laughed and said,

"Tell the teacher. I dare you."

I was frightened by her, and I sat there quietly as she copied the answers from my paper. I spent many hours researching and getting the answers, and in five minutes, she had copied them and would receive a good grade off of my hard work. I was so afraid of being physically hurt that I took the mental abuse because in my mind, it was better for *Lauren* to copy my paper than for me to risk getting beaten up later.

One night while doing my homework, I angrily slammed my book closed and threw it on the floor. Why did I have to be so smart? I knew I was smart because I studied hard, took good notes in class, and went the extra mile to produce quality work. It seemed like the higher grades I made, the more my classmates ridiculed me, and I was sick of it! I got up from my desk, kicked my textbook across the floor and made a decision that night not to study anymore. Perhaps if I achieved lower scores, I would be bullied less and could finally fit in with my classmates. This was a dumb decision and deep down inside, I knew it was dumb, but I was so desperate to make the madness end that I was willing to do anything for a reprieve, even fail.

The next day in my social studies class, my teacher, Mrs. Stallings, passed out a test. I was not prepared for it at all because I barely studied the night before. The old Tensie who made it her mission to know the test material backwards and forward, this time knew nothing. Out of a 30 question test, I knew less than half the material, if that. The sad part was that I did not feel panic or shame for not studying. Instead, I felt a sense of relief because I knew I would not do well on the test and would finally be able to fit in.

A few days later, I received my grade back: it was a 58. When Mrs. Stallings handed back my paper, she had a look of shock and disbelief on her face and asked me to see her after class. My black classmates around me asked,

"Tensie, what you get?" I said, "a 58, you?"

They smiled and high-fived me. One person said, "Alright, you failed like me. Congratulations!" and she started laughing. At that moment, I smiled, too, because for once in my life, I was fitting in. This time, the students did not laugh or tease me because I made an A, nor did they snatch my paper to see the grade I made when I refused to show them. They were proud of me for failing, and for the rest of the day, my life was easier. Some of my white classmates were shocked that I failed, but I was not concerned with what they thought. I was just happy to finally be fitting in. The black students who failed even asked me to walk with them to their next class. For the rest of the day, I did not have to worry about being called a nerd, goody-two-shoes, sell-out, or fear being pushed into a locker.

Instead, they applauded me and welcomed me into their circle. It felt great to fit in.

The euphoria I felt was short-lived because eventually, I had to face my parents. My parents took a great interest in my academics and knew exactly what was going on in my classes. During family dinner that night, Mom asked,

"How was school? Did you get your social studies test back yet?"

I had two choices: I could tell the truth and face the consequences or I could try and hide the test from her. Since Mom worked at Terrell Lane Middle School, option two was out of the question. I knew Mrs. Stallings could easily tell her about my failing grade, and I did not want Mom to find out that way. After dinner, I went to my book bag and pulled out my test. With fear in my eyes, hands trembling, and sweaty palms, I handed Mom my test. She loudly yelled,

"WHAT?!" "What in the world did you do wrong?" Her reaction made me flinch.

By this time, Dad walked over to look at my test paper and asked,

"Janine, what happened?"

Shamefully, I looked at them, slowly shrugged my shoulders and replied,

"I don't know. I guess I didn't study hard enough."

"Based on this grade, it looks like you didn't study at all. You know your father and I tell you to always do your best, and this is not your best. You were bringing home high A's, even 100s, and now you are failing. I am going to say this once and only once: you *better* not bring another failing grade again in this house, you hear me? Go to your room, do your homework, and study." My mother shouted.

I respectfully did as I was told and with tears in my eyes, I ran to my room to begin doing my homework. The look on my parents' faces, as well as hearing them say how disappointed they were in me stung worse than if I had been spanked with Mom's flip flop. They worked so hard to provide for me and give me a good life, and realizing that I let them down made me feel guilty.

From that moment on, I vowed to never bring home a failing grade nor would I deliberately try to fail, just to fit in with the crowd. I realized how blessed I was to have parents who cared about me, exercised tough love to ensure I did well academically, and got me back on track when I needed it. What I later learned is that my classmates who picked on me did not have parents who were concerned about their academic success. If they brought home a failing grade, their parent(s) probably did not scold them or demand better from them. The parent probably did not even know the child had a test and failed. Gratefully, my parents were very involved in my academic affairs.

The next day, I turned my signed paper in with a letter to my teacher. She talked with me and asked the same question Mom had,

"What happened?"

I was too embarrassed to tell her that I had deliberately failed, so I made up a quick excuse,

"I'm not sure. I think I froze and forgot the material. I promise to do better next time and this won't happen again." Thinking I had gotten off scotch free with the quick excuse, her response let me know that teachers are more insightful and observant than most students realize.

"You are one of my best students Tensie. I've noticed that some of your classmates have been talking to you and distracting you from your work. To make sure this doesn't happen again, I am moving you to the front of the class."

"Yes ma'am." I replied feeling relieved, knowing that I would be closer to the teacher and farther away from the students' rude and demeaning comments. I felt less pressure and my academic confidence and good grades returned. Students no longer grabbed my test papers or demanded I show them my grades on an assignment. Being at the front was a different world, a better world, and I was in a much happier and peaceful place.

My grades and behavior went back to normal, and I never once thought about failing again. Honestly, it took too much work to act dumb. Even though I felt revered by my classmates who said it was cool to be dumb, that feeling quickly faded. According to some of my black peers, to do well academically was to equate myself with being white and a sellout. If excelling meant I would be a sell out, then I sold right on. I became my old self again, and the snarky comments about my academic ability returned. It was tough to be picked on, but I thought to myself: *Why am I changing who I am to fit in with a group of people who treat me cruelly and despise success?* This was not the circle I wanted to be in. I only wanted to surround myself with positive individuals who uplifted one another, not brought people down.

I often pondered how my life would have been different if my teacher had never moved me to the front of the class or if my parents had not implemented tough love and made sure I performed well in school. I understand why some young people fall prey to performing poorly in school. Peer pressure is real, and when a person does not have a support system at home, life can be more complicated. Although I thought I was cool by failing in school, my parents quickly yanked me back to reality and my academic progress improved. I thank God for my loving, caring, and concerned parents. They kept me on the right path to success.

Chapter 6

Slightly Hardheaded

At times, I was slightly hardheaded and did not always heed the advice of my parents. The threat Mom gave me about making sure I did well in school echoed in my mind. My parents told me that when I went to school, I was to do two things and two things only: (1) to learn and (2) to behave. I learned well and was on my best behavior because I knew that if I were not, not only would I be reprimanded at school, but I would also be punished at home. In order to avoid either forms of punishment, I was on my best behavior, for the most part.

The bullying I experienced at school began to lessen slightly because I began taking honors classes. Oftentimes, I was the only black student in these classes, and my white classmates never bullied or called me mean names like some of my black classmates did. The white students befriended me.

One particular day in my Algebra class, my teacher, Mrs. McNamara, asked me to run an errand for her.

"Tensie, please take this letter to Ms. Kemp and come right back." Mrs. McNamara said.

"Yes ma'am. I'll be right back." I replied.

Needless to say, I did not come right back. After I dropped off the letter, I saw a friend in the hallway and started talking to her for several minutes. Ten minutes later, I was still in the hallway talking and my teacher began looking for me. Mrs. McNamara found me in the hallway and told me to come to class immediately. Not wanting to be disrespectful and recognizing I was in the wrong, I apologized, ended my conversation abruptly, and walked back to class.

A few minutes after returning to class, a classmate who sat in front of me turned around and started talking to me. I knew I was not supposed to talk in class, but I felt special that she was talking to me instead of picking on me. Normally, the only time *Kasey* said something to me was to tell me how big my eyes looked. *Kasey* was a popular student and was known for her athletic abilities. Students liked her and no one ever picked on her. She and I were two of few blacks in the Honors Algebra class. However, this time, *Kasey* said hello to me and asked about a math problem.

I began talking to her and felt relieved that she was not making fun of my eyes. Mrs. McNamara heard us talking and said, "Shhh!" *Kasey* turned around in her seat and went back to working on her math problem. A few minutes later, I tapped her on the shoulder, and we began talking again. My teacher walked back to us and said,

"If I have to tell you two to be quiet again, you both are going to the office."

We immediately ended our conversation and finished working on our assignment before the bell rang to release us for the day. A feeling of solitude and pride came over me. I had successfully made it through the day without anyone bullying me, and *Kasey*—who typically had negative things to say to me—actually wanted to talk to me. Things were looking up.

When I got home that evening, I heard Mom on the phone finishing up a conversation,

"Thank you for calling us. We appreciate this and will make sure we speak to Tensie."

I suddenly stopped in my tracks and my heart began to beat rapidly. Mrs. McNamara had called my parents because I was misbehaving in class, twice. At that moment, I hoped and prayed I would be stricken with some illness and have to be rushed to the hospital. This was the only way I was going to escape the inevitable. I did not want Mom to get off the phone.

A few minutes later, even though it felt like an eternity, Mom hung up the phone and yelled,

"Jannnniiiiiinnnnneee, come here! Now!"

I slowly walked to the kitchen as if I were going to be executed. I now understood how John Coffee felt on his walk to the electric chair in *The Green Mile*. My life was about to become electrocuted by my mother's lecture and probably her flip flop. My thoughts were interrupted when Mom asked,

"Guess who that was on the phone?"

Even though I knew, I surprisingly said, "I have no idea. Who?"

She said, "It was Mrs. McNamara. She has noticed changes in your behavior at school and felt it was time to have a phone call. Why were you wandering the halls at school and talking in class, even after she asked you to stop?"

The shame I had previously felt for purposefully failing my test came back to me once again. I replied,

"I don't know. My classmate asked a question about a math problem and I tried to help her."

"How many times have I told you that your father and I send you to school to learn? You do your work, get good grades, and behave. You do not give your teachers any trouble. You are not behaving. What has gotten into you?"

I did not share with her that it felt good to go to school for one day without being bullied or how special I felt to have a classmate talk to me without making fun of my appearance. I kept these stories to myself and promised her I would do better. Because I had gotten in trouble one time too many, as I predicted, I got a spanking that night with the infamous flip flop. Although that flip flop hurt, it motivated me more than ever to get my act together and to get it together quickly. My mother had me apologize to Mrs. McNamara the next day, and I told her I would not disrupt her class again. This incident happened only one time in her class because my parents were stern, yet fair. I was fortunate to have only gotten away with a spanking, and I was not going to take my chances and see what would happen next if I misbehaved again. I am not sure why I did not tell Mom about the bullying at school, but as things continued to get worse, I would later share with my parents all that was transpiring, and they would take matters into their own hands.

Chapter 7

Don't Mess with My Mama

I tried to remain as optimistic as possible, despite the constant bullying I faced. I vacillated whether or not I should tell my parents about what was happening at school because on one hand, it might alleviate the torment I was experiencing at school, but on the other hand, it might make matters worse. After debating with myself for several days, I decided that it was time to tell Mom.

I told Mom when I was ten years old and in the fifth grade; she was the librarian at Laurel Mill Elementary School, and everyone loved her. She had a beautiful personality, strong work ethic, a creative nature, and a heart of gold. She implemented many programs at Laurel Mill, such as Character Dress up Day and Storytelling Day. People described Mom as a very nice and sweet lady. She smiled all the time, gave hugs, and had an infectious and funny laugh. To hear her laugh made others laugh.

Still fearful that telling on my bullies would end in a negative situation, I decided to tell Mom only about my main bully *Lauren*. One fall afternoon as we were walking out of school and getting into the car, I blurted out,

"Mom, *Lauren* is bullying me at school."

Mom stopped putting on her seatbelt, looked at me, and said,

"What?!"

"I'm afraid to go to school. You've seen her. She is much taller and bigger than me, and she picks on me relentlessly. She makes fun of my clothes, shoes, and eyes. Several times, she stole my paper off my desk and copied my work. She even threatened to hurt me if I did not give her my homework. But most recently, when I refused to open the door for her to the locker room, she grabbed my arm from behind, bent it back as hard as she could, trying to break it. The only way I got her to stop was by screaming and yelling. She stopped for fear that our gym teacher heard me." I said.

By this time, Mom was furious. She angrily buckled her seatbelt, forcefully put the key in the ignition, and began talking hurriedly as she drove home.

"I can't believe she has been hurting MY baby! You did the right thing by telling me. How dare she pick on you?" Mom gave an angry chuckle. "She messed with the wrong one. I might be nice, but when someone puts her hands on my child, that's a different story! You don't worry about anything Janine. She will not and I repeat will NOT get away with this. I will deal with her tomorrow."

That night at dinner, Mom shared with Dad what I told her. He echoed Mom's sentiments and said that *Lauren* needed to be dealt with. After doing my homework and getting ready for bed, I felt calmer that night. I felt good knowing that Mom would deal with the situation, but I still felt nervous.

The next day in Mr. McLaughlin's class, the secretary buzzed in on the intercom,

"Mr. McLaughlin, please send *Lauren* to the library. Thank You."

When I heard these words, I froze because I knew what was about to happen. My heart began to beat thunderously, and I was so terribly scared that my palms started sweating. My attention was diverted from my school work and I had lost all focus.

A range of emotions ran through me. I began to get angry at myself for telling Mom. I just knew this situation would end up disastrously. Instead of trusting Mom and thinking positively that after this conversation, things would get better, I focused only on the negative and thought that only the worst could happen. I was sure things would backfire.

Approximately forty minutes later, *Lauren* returned to class. She looked absolutely miserable. Her eyes were red, and she kept her head down when she walked back into class. I could tell she had been crying. As she took her seat, I kept my head low to avoid eye contact with her, hoping to appear invisible.

"Tensie?"

I heard *Lauren* call my name, and I pretended like I did not hear her. She called my name again.

"Tensie?"

I finally looked up with scared, fearful, and timid eyes. *Lauren* said, "I'm sorry."

She then put her head on her desk and kept her gaze downward. I stared in amazement. Did my ears just deceive me? Did she really apologize to me? I was still awestruck, yet felt a sense of pride. For the rest of my fifth grade year, my life was a little easier. *Lauren* did not say very much to me, nor did she pick on me. I stayed out of her way and she stayed out of mine. I was glad to no longer have to deal with her verbal and physical torments that it wasn't until a few days later when I asked Mom how she worked her magic.

"Mom?" I asked.

"*Lauren* hasn't bothered me at school since you talked to her. What exactly did you say?"

"When she came into the library, I politely asked her to come into my office. Once in my office, I closed my door and laid her soul out! I told her that she had BETTER leave you alone and that I wasn't playing with her. Even though she was taller than me, I had her stand up and, I looked her dead in the eye, and told her that if she did anything, ANYTHING, else to you, she was going to deal with me, and it would not be pretty! I showed her I meant business!"

After hearing this, I started laughing and proudly said, "Go Mom! Thank you!" Mom shared with me that *Lauren* even started crying.

"Are you serious?! Big bad *Lauren*? The girl who yelled at me for screaming when she tried to break my arm? The girl who stole my paper off my desk and copied my work? The girl who threw a kickball at me

during recess? This girl is the one who started crying??"
I asked unbelievingly.

"Yes ma'am, that's the one." Mom said.

My immediate reaction was laughter. I began to
laugh hysterically because I pictured her crying like a
baby. The thought of her wiping her eyes and sniveling
like an infant gave me great euphoria. It wasn't that I
felt good because she was miserable and crying, but it
felt great to know that she cried. She wasn't as bad as
she portrayed to be and perhaps if I had stood up to
her, I could have shut her down.

The image of me standing on a chair and pointing
my finger in her face and yelling at her didn't quite have
the same effect as Mom's story. I pictured *Lauren*
flipping the chair over and seeing my small self collapse
to the ground. I did the right thing by telling Mom, and
I was proud of myself for mustering up enough courage
to tell her what I had been experiencing at school.
Because of it, I had a reprieve from being bullied.

In one instance when someone tried to say
something mean to me, *Lauren* actually stood up for me
and said, "Leave her alone." As the school year
progressed, and we came to the library during Black
History Month, I sat down at a table, and the next thing
I knew, *Lauren* sat across from me. I was in disbelief
and a little scared because I was not sure if she was
sitting down to torture me or to be nice. To my
surprise, she acted decently towards me, and I even
helped her with her Black History Project. I might not

have been brave enough to stand up for myself, but I had my Mom on my side, and that was all that mattered. Don't mess with my mama!

Chapter 8

Big-Eyed Freak

We all have something we do not like about our physical appearance, whether it is our height, weight, nose, chest size, or another imperfection, we recognize that we are not flawless and some people try desperately to correct their imperfections. Ever since I was four years old, I have been self-conscious about my eyes. I have big eyes, a trait I inherited from Dad. As a child I noticed that my siblings, Jemonde and Kelise, had "normal" sized eyes, but mine just seemed so much bigger. I constantly wondered why I was the only child to take after my Dad's eyes, and I began to hate them because my eyes became the brunt of many endless mean jokes.

During my elementary, middle, and high school years, students made cruel comments about my eyes. However, I received the most torment during high school. Names like frog, GEICO Direct, and big-eyed freak were taunts I heard daily. Even though fellow classmates were well aware of my name, they preferred to call me animal names and cartoon characters instead. One student remarked that I looked like Beetle juice and another person said,

"As big as your eyes are, I bet you can see the whole world with your eyes closed."

I even had a bully ask me almost daily,

"Why are your eyes so big? It kind of scares me when you look at me." To hear these comments daily took a toll on my self-esteem, and I became ashamed to look at people in the face for fear of what they would say next about the size of my eyes.

During my ninth grade year at Louisburg High School in my computer class, one student relentlessly said,

"Tensie, stop looking at me! You are scaring me with those big eyes."

Whenever he made this remark, people around him started laughing. I tried to laugh it off, but inwardly, it bothered me so much. I had become so self-conscious about my eyes that I began walking around with my eyes squinted or wore shades outside every chance I got, even when it was cloudy. I had a friend remark to me,

"You would be pretty if your eyes weren't so big." That comment stung.

At 14 years old, I was beginning to experiment with make-up. I noticed my sister Kelise lining her eyes with a black pencil. After she finished, I was mesmerized by how beautiful it made her look and how smaller her eyes appeared.

"What's that called?" I asked inquisitively.

"It's eyeliner," she said.

"May I try it?" I asked.

"Sure," she replied.

I meticulously watched her and studied her hand movements as she lined her eye. I began practicing and noticed that the thicker I made my eyeliner, the smaller my eyes looked. I even learned that by lining my top and bottom eyelids, my eyes looked even smaller. Bingo! I had discovered a way to make my eyes appear smaller. My plan was quickly shifted when Mom walked in.

"What is that mess on your eyes?" Mom asked.

"It is black eyeliner, and I think it looks pretty." I replied.

"Take it off now. It's way too heavy and you look like Cleopatra. You have naturally pretty eyes. You don't need to put that on. Take it off."

Being obedient, I removed the eye makeup and was heartbroken that I could not wear it.

I was in the Louisburg High School marching band, and I played the trumpet. I had been playing trumpet since the sixth grade and was inspired by my brother Jemonde because he is an excellent trumpeter. I had a love/hate relationship with my band class because it was such a big class, and many students were in it. I loved playing the trumpet, but I hated being around so many people because I knew somebody would have something mean to say about me. A name that stands out the most from band class is *Angie*. *Angie* was a black female who played a brass instrument in the band. Her hair always looked a mess at school, as if she never combed it. She thought it was funny to call me GEICO Direct because of my big eyes.

Each day in marching band, she yelled,

"Hey GEICO!" The first few times this happened, students laughed and asked her why she called me that. She said,

"Because she got big eyes." From then on, other students started calling me this name. I hated *Angie* for embarrassing me, and I detested her for making fun of something I could not control. During warm ups, *Angie* loudly said,

"Where's GEICO? GEICO Direct, where are you?" People started laughing and remarked, "She really does look like a gecko because of her big eyes. How scary."

I went from being bullied for wearing non name-brand clothes, bullied for being academically successful, bullied for being small, and now I was being bullied because of my eyes. When would the meanness end? Sometimes, I tried to find a friend, hoping to get the attention off of me, but *Angie* always found a way to make me visible to people when I wanted to be invisible.

I went home every night and cried myself to sleep because I hated my eyes. I used the slow, dial-up in my parents' house to research various sources on the web to figure out how I could have eye surgery to reduce my eye size. I knew that when I became an adult, I would find a plastic surgeon to reduce my eye size. In addition, I researched "How to make big eyes look small" on Yahoo because any advice I could find to help make me look normal, I wanted. I was willing to risk my eyesight and possibly my health to make my eyes look small. That's how desperate I was.

Since I was too young to wear eyeliner and I could not have reconstructive eye surgery, I thought of another way. Before crying myself to sleep most nights, I placed a picture of my sister under my pillow and prayed to God to make my eyes normal like hers.

I prayed: *Dear God, thank You for waking me up this morning and for allowing me to have clothes on my back and food on my table. Please continue to bless my family and everyone in the world. God, I am asking You to do me a huge favor. Please make my eyes normal like my sister. I am tired of getting picked on and bullied for having big eyes. If You can please make my eyes normal like hers, I will love You forever. I have even placed her picture under my pillow to show You how her eyes look. These and all other blessings I ask in Your name, Amen.*

For four years, I prayed this prayer each night before I went to bed and each morning, I eagerly woke up, ran to the mirror, and checked my eyes, hoping they would be smaller. When I looked at myself, I was terribly disappointed; they were still big. I felt betrayed and angry at God for not making my eyes smaller and for making me be born this way. I told Him that if I had normal eyes, students at school would not pick on me so profusely. I was small, skinny, had no shape, and flat-chested, and now kids were bullying me for being a big-eyed freak. What was the point of going on with life?

As the school year progressed, a student in my band class, named *Dominika*, started picking on me. *Dominika* was extremely overweight and began calling me GEICO Direct, too. I found her behavior ironic because she was being picked on for her weight, and yet, she made fun of me because of the size of my eyes. I presumed she acted this way because she was relieved that the attention was no longer on her.

During band class, *Dominika* said, "GEICO. GEICO GEICOOOO." I tried to ignore her and pretended I did not hear her, but when I did not turn around, she raised her voice louder, which made the students around her laugh even harder. I finally turned around and said,

"What?"

She looked at me and started laughing hysterically. I was taken aback by her behavior. Constantly, she faced criticism from her peers, and people bullied her because of her obesity, and yet, she had the audacity to make fun of my eyes? Instead of joining in with the jeers and taunts from students, she could have been an ally to me, and I an ally to her, and together, we could have helped put a stop to those who bullied us.

One hot, humid, August day during band class, I was cranky, in a foul mood, and sick of being called GEICO. When *Dominika* called me the name that day, I angrily turned around and said,

"Look! You're one to talk. I'd rather have big eyes than be fat like you! At least the only thing big on my body are my eyes. Too bad you can't say the same!"

This was the second time in my life that I stood up for myself to a bully. Immediately, people started laughing at my comment, and she hung her head in embarrassment. It felt good to stand up to *Dominika,* and I felt no shame for making that comment. She had been calling me this name for months, so I felt I was justified in making my comment.

As band class ended and we rushed back to the band room, I saw *Dominika* walk with her head down. I am not a mean person, and my parents did not raise me to be that way. They instilled in me to treat people with dignity and respect. Even though she probably deserved that comment for always making fun of me, it was not right for me to retaliate and be mean to her. I had knots in my stomach, and I felt awful for what I said. I also empathized with her because she was being bullied about her weight.

I ran up behind her, *"Dominika, Dominika,* I am sorry for my comment. I should not have made fun of your weight, but I get so tired of you calling me GEICO that I went off. How about this, you don't call me GEICO Direct and I won't say anything else about your size. Deal?" She replied, "Deal" and apologized for making fun of me.

After that encounter, she never called me GEICO again. I wish I could say the same for *Angie*. Up until my senior year of high school, *Angie* continued to call me GEICO Direct and the sad part is, I let her. Perhaps if I had tried talking to her as I had done with *Dominika*, she may have stopped. The reason I never stood up to *Angie* was because she was part of a clique, and if I had said or done something to her, I knew my life would be more miserable because her clique would come after me. *Dominika* did not have many friends, and I knew if I said something to her, she would not have an entourage beat me up. Then again, maybe if I had said something to *Angie*, she might have stopped making fun of me.

It is because of *Angie's* and *Dominika's* comments and hurtful words from other students that I suffered so much. There were times when I wanted to poke my eyes with a needle hoping they would bleed so much and become smaller. This idea was absolutely ridiculous, but I was so depressed and desperate that I was willing to do anything, even jeopardize my eyesight. Imagine being so self-conscious and not wanting to talk to people because of fear of what they might say about your eyes. How ironic that I walked around with squinted eyes trying to be seen as normal, but people commented,

"Why are you walking around looking crazy? Open your eyes!" I even had a parent ask me,

"Why do you keep your eyes squinted?"

My mother told me, "Stop squinting and open up your eyes. You have beautiful eyes and should not be ashamed of them." I paid Mom's words no attention because she was my mother and was supposed to say nice things, or so I thought.

Even when I rode the bus home in the afternoons in high school, students continued making fun of my eyes. I sat in the front of the bus and stayed to myself, when a student at the back of the bus yelled,

"Squirrel!"

I ignored the name because I did not think anyone was talking to me. Yet, the name calling continued,

"Squirrel! Squirrel! Turn around, I know you hear me!" By this time, several students started giggling, and I got the uneasy feeling that she was talking to me. A few seconds later, I felt something hit the back of my head. It was a bag of potato chips, and the whole bus erupted in laughter. The girl calling me "squirrel" had thrown food at me, and it hit me in the back of my head. She went on to say,

"Squirrel, I know you hear me talking to you!"

Trying to hold back the tears, I turned around and looked at her.

"Yea, YOU. You don't recognize your name? You look like a squirrel with your big eyes." She meanly said. People kept laughing, and I turned back around in my seat.

The guy sitting behind me asked, "Why you let her talk to you like that? You should say something back."

I replied, "No, it's not worth it."

I did not say anything back because I was afraid. This girl was bigger than me and had a reputation for getting in fights. I did not want her to beat me up. I thought to myself, *why doesn't this guy stand up for me and tell her to stop? He heard her calling me 'squirrel,' and yet he didn't do or say anything.* Again, no one came to my rescue, and I continued my bus ride home listening to her call me squirrel. It was becoming harder and harder to fight back the tears.

It would not be until four years later during my freshman year of college at North Carolina State University that I would receive my first compliment about my eyes. When I received that compliment, my confidence slowly began to increase. And later, when I saw the talented actress Traci Ellis Ross on television and saw how big and beautiful her eyes were, my shame of having big eyes slowly started to dissipate.

Chapter 9

IBTC

My entire life, I have been small. I am twenty eight years old at the time of this book's publication, and I have never weighed more than 113 pounds. People tell me they would kill to be my size. But being small is not as lovely as it seems. In school, I was short and skinny, and today, I am a whopping 5 feet 1 inch tall. Because I am small, people felt privileged to make comments. "Why are you so skinny? Do you ever eat? Girl, you need to put some meat on dem bones." I heard this all the time, and these comments aggravated me.

In school, I noticed that guys were attracted to girls who had big breasts, big behinds or as they called them, *thick chicks*. In their words, they preferred mashed potatoes, and I was a string bean. I was tiny and flat-chested and guys were not attracted to me because I didn't have a figure. I abhorred changing for PE class, and I tried to find a spot where no one could see me change. The girls who changed clothes were B, C, and D cups. Just as I made A's in all my classes, I was an A in bra size. When I changed for PE class, I put my shirt on as quickly as possible before anyone made a comment about my flat chest. Sometimes it worked, other times it did not.

Since I was not "well endowed" as Mom called it, she bought me bras that had padding to give an illusion that I had a little something up top. I also wanted something to poke through my shirt, but people still made fun of me for having a small chest. Guys told me that I probably shopped in the bra section for children and was a member of the IBTC.

"What's IBTC?" I asked one guy.

"It's the Itty Bitty Titty Committee," he said, and people roared in laughter. On several occasions, guys and girls said they could not tell my front from my back and if I stood sideways, I might just disappear. Some students said my chest was so small that I probably looked like a man with my shirt off or my breasts were the size of two mosquito bites. The taunts kept coming.

One afternoon after PE class, a group of girls sat near me and began discussing different types of bras they wore: sports bra, regular bra, and push up bra. One girl looked me up and down and said,

"Too bad Tensie don't know what we talking about. She probably don't even wear a bra cuz she ain't got nothin' to hold up."

People sitting near us began laughing, and I felt mortified. I turned red as a beet and began questioning God again. Why had He made me with big eyes, skinny, and no chest?

My mind began thinking, and I was reminded of an episode of the Fresh Prince of Bel Air (my all-time favorite show) in Season 3, episode 3 when Ashley stuffed her bra with tissue to get guys' attention at school, and it worked. Brilliant! I thought this was a genius idea.

When I got home that afternoon, I grabbed a box of tissues and began stuffing my bra. After I finished, I looked at the result in the mirror. One breast looked like the end of an ice cream cone—pointy and long—and the other breast looked like I had been stung by a bumble bee. They were heavily uneven and lop-sized and looked plain terrible. If I went to school like that, I really would be the laughing stock of the school. Plus, Mom would have noticed and made me take out that ridiculous stuffing; I was not going to school looking like who did it and why.

It perplexed me why people were so cruel. Why did students feel the need to always make fun of me? If they wanted to compare chest sizes or talk about various types of bras, they could have done so without making me the center of their jokes. Yet, they went out of their way to deliberately tease me and make fun of my imperfections. The more students knew their words affected me, the more they continued to pick on me. I became self-conscious again and walked around with my arms crossed trying to hide my deflated front and wore a jacket, sometimes even in warm weather, to cover up my nonexistent chest. Anything I could do to divert their attention from me, I did.

What I found most interesting is that students were creative in making up jokes about me, but were failing their classes. They did not know what a simile was, but they used several by saying that my chest was as small as a mosquito bite. If only they could have used their creativity for good and focused on their grades, they might have actually graduated from high school or done something productive with their lives. Instead, they were so insecure about themselves that they tried to bring me down in order to bring themselves up.

During my freshman year of high school, we took a band trip to play at a contest in Florida. I had dozed off to sleep and woke up to get my blanket because the air conditioning was blasting on the bus. I stood up to reach the overhead compartment, as someone from the back of the bus yelled,

"Hey Tensie, somebody back here said you look like a fake Barbie doll."

Immediately as if a light switch had been flipped on, people started laughing. I grabbed my blanket, ignored their comments, and sat back down trying not to cry. My seatmate told me to pay them no attention because they were immature. I tried my hardest to ignore that comment, but the words stung deeply.

I sat for the rest of the trip glued to my seat until we arrived at the hotel in Florida. I had to use the bathroom badly, but I held it in for hours because I did not want to get up and use the bathroom. The students who made the comment about me being a fake Barbie doll were at the back of the bus, and I had to pass them to get to the bathroom. I was so fearful of what they would say next about me that I stayed put. Once we pulled up to the hotel in Florida, we were given our room assignments, and I ran to my room, used the restroom, and unpacked. After I unpacked, I put on my bathing suit, threw a towel around me, and headed to the pool. I loved swimming, but I was very self-conscious about the smallness of my body. I shopped long and hard trying to find a bathing suit that for the most part, covered me up and gave me a little padding in the chest area. I found one that I thought was suitable, and I faced my fears, took off my towel, and walked towards the shallow end of the pool. Before I got in, a student remarked,

"Hey ya'll, look at this skeleton getting in the water."

Everybody burst out laughing. I stood there like a deer in headlights, wanting to turn around, run to my room, and cry, but I knew that if I did, the students would say something else. So, I smacked my lips, tried to laugh along with them, and waded in the pool. I only stayed for a few minutes because the students were playing too roughly with each other. They were being loud and obnoxious and guys were grabbing girls and throwing them in the pool, even if they could not swim. I did not feel comfortable or safe around these individuals because who knew what they might try to do to me? They already did not like me and if they were throwing people in the pool, they might have harmed me. I knew how to swim, but I did not want to take any chances. All it would take was for one person to play around and hold my head under water or try to accidentally drown me, and I would be no more. I got out of the pool, put my towel on, and went back to my room. I was not going to let them hurt me.

Chapter 10

Teaching Stuffed Animals

In Charles Dickens' *A Tale of Two Cities*, he remarked, "It was the best of times, it was the worst of times." These twelve words describe exactly how I felt when I went to school. There were times when I successfully made it through a day without a bully picking on me, saying something mean to me, or physically abusing me. No matter what I experienced at school, my saving grace was knowing that when I came home, I was safe and loved. I came home to an environment where people encouraged me and did not criticize me, asked me what grade I received without demeaning me, and hugged me instead of pushed me. My home was a safe haven.

I enthusiastically looked forward to coming home every afternoon to line up my stuffed animals and teach them the material I learned in school that day. Teaching runs in my family because my parents were teachers before they retired, and I learned techniques and information on how to effectively teach from them. I enjoyed teaching my stuffed animals because they were incredibly cute and cuddly and because they could not verbally or physically bully me like my classmates did at school. My stuffed animals listened to my problems, heard my bullying stories, hugged me, and slept snugly next to me as I cried myself to sleep many nights. They were like my family, and I treated them as such. I had more than thirty stuffed animals that consisted of bears, cats, birds, dogs, seals, and puppies. I even gave several of my favorite stuffed animals names such as Blubur, Mr. Seals, Care Bear, Tweety, and Fluffy. When no one else was there for me, I could count on them to be there.

When I came home from school, I ran into my room and immediately brought my stuffed animals into the library of my parents' house, a room we called the study. I lined them up and arranged them by height and size. The smaller and shorter ones—like me—sat in the front of the room, while the bigger animals sat in the back. I made sure each animal saw properly and that nobody's big head obstructed their view. Because Tweety Bird's head was huge, he always sat in the back, which did not seem to bother him because he sat quietly during class. I arranged my animals this way because I knew how it felt to be small and short and not see the board, and I wanted to make sure each animal had the same and equal opportunity to learn and do well.

"Good Afternoon class. I hope your day is going well. I have written out today's agenda on the board, and we will follow it accordingly. First, let's begin by taking roll."

I began calling each of my stuffed animals' names and used some of my classmates' names from school. I pointed to the chalkboard my parents bought me and made sure each animal addressed me properly by calling me Ms. Taylor. I taught different subjects ranging from

English and Mathematics to Science and Social Studies. The information I taught my "students," was the information I learned that day from school. Not only did I teach my animals, but this process helped me retain the lessons I learned in school, which helped my academic performance even more.

I began taking roll. "*John. Jesse. Megan. Jane. Giselle. Brielle. Thomas. Rudolph. Serenity.*" Each student said here or present and for those who did not answer this way and tried to be funny, I made them say it again until they had addressed me properly. After role had been taken and all students were present, I started my lesson.

On this day, I decided to teach mathematics.

"*John*, what is twelve times eight?" I asked. He looked at me confusedly and replied,

"I don't know."

I walked over to *John* who is really my Tweety Bird stuffed animal, and said,

"I beg your pardon? Did you even try? Put your pencil to the paper and work out this math problem."

"Ok, ok!" he exclaimed. He scribbled the problem down on his paper and tried to solve it. "Twelve times eight is 96."

"Very good!" I exclaimed. I always made sure to give my "students" praise. Often times, teachers only recognize students when they misbehave or perform poorly in school, but I found the balance. I encouraged my students and congratulated them for good work and great behavior, while still whipping them into shape when they misbehaved. In my class, students got rewarded for getting a correct answer, even if I simply told them, "Nice job!"

John was smiling because he got the correct answer. By this time, I noticed *Giselle* standing up and talking to a classmate.

"*Giselle*, sit down and shut up!" I yelled. "You are disrupting my class and the learning environment for everyone else."

This only made things worse. I then noticed that *Megan* and *Jesse* were passing notes to each other. I walked over to them and said,

"Excuse me? Is there something else you'd rather be doing than learning? I see you two passing each other notes like you're delivering mail."

"This is boring Ms. Taylor. I don't wanna learn this." *Megan* and *Jesse* said.

"Well you have two choices. One, you can either sit here, shut your mouth, open your text book, and learn or two, you can go to the principal's office for disrupting my class. But what you won't do is continue to pass notes and disrupt my class. Which option do you prefer?"

Megan and *Jesse* did not say anything. They quickly closed their mouths, stopped passing notes, and began astutely working on their math problems. What an imagination I had! My stuffed animals never truly opened their mouths to speak, nor did they catch an attitude with me, or even blink their eyes for that matter. Instead, they kept their eyes straight and had big warm smiles on their faces, some with huge teeth. I personified them.

What I lacked in having the gusto to say at school for fear of getting pushed around or teased, I made up for by disciplining my stuffed animal students and making sure they were well behaved and excelled in my class. No one and I mean no one was bullied in my class of stuffed animals. Nobody called anyone a vicious name nor did anyone pick on another individual for being small or for performing well academically because I made sure of it. Many times, my parents would hear me yelling at my students, and Mom said to Dad,

"Whoo weee, I declare Janine has a bad class!"

At least three times a week, a stuffed animal was getting yelled at to sit down, shut up, or get out of my class. I had a Zero Tolerance policy for disrespect. I was small, but feisty. Either the students came to my class to learn or they risked getting embarrassed in front of their friends by being yelled at, sent to the principal's office, or going to In-School Suspension (ISS). In rare occasions, a few students received a spanking with a flip flop (oh the irony), and after I spanked them once, I never had to discipline them again. As the school year continued, and the students realized that I was a tough cookie, they finally got their act together, became respectful to me and their other classmates, and my class became stellar with students making A's and B's in both school work and conduct.

English was my favorite subject to teach. I excelled at this subject because Dad was an exceptional English teacher, as evidenced by statements and comments made from his students. He taught me everything I needed to learn in school and for my class at home. He taught me new vocabulary words, how to diagram sentences, the different parts of speech (i.e. noun, verb, adjective, adverb, conjunction, participle). In addition to having a great English teacher for a Dad, I increased my skills by watching the show, School House Rock. Because of this show, I learned how to correctly differentiate between using an adjective and adverb in a sentence.

"This afternoon class, we are going to learn about adjectives and adverbs. Does anyone know the difference between the two?" The room fell silent and no one's hand went up. I continued with my lesson.

"An adjective modifies a noun or pronoun and describes a person, place, or thing. An adverb modifies verbs and clauses and sometimes other adjectives and adverbs. To help you remember the two, keep in mind that adverbs answer the question how and are normally followed by the verb. They also end in -ly"

"Let's try an example." I wrote the following sentence on the chalkboard: Johnny played the trumpet wonderfully.

"*Megan*, what is the adverb in the sentence? Remember, adverbs follow the verb, ask how, and often end in -ly."

Megan mouthed the sentence to herself and began to ponder. After a few seconds, she said,

"Ms. Taylor, the adverb is wonderfully."

"Very good *Megan*! Wonderfully is the adverb because it describes how he played. You wouldn't say Johnny played wonderful because in that case wonderful would be an adjective and not an adverb. Let's break the sentence down even further. *Jane*, tell me what each part of speech is."

Jane wrote down the sentence on her paper and began to diagram it.

"Ms. Taylor, Johnny is the subject, played is the verb, trumpet is the noun and direct object, and wonderfully is the adverb."

I walked over to her and gave her a high five.

"Excelsior!" I exclaimed. I heard Dad use this word often to describe the work of an outstanding student in his class. "You got it!" I was proud of my class because they were listening to the lesson and grasping English extremely well.

I made sure my students understood the material. I went over many examples in class, walked them through several concepts, and before I tested them, I made sure they felt comfortable with all the material I was teaching. I also told them that if they did not understand a lesson I was teaching, they could stay after class to learn more until they officially grasped the material.

As a student, I had a penchant and strong love for teaching, and as much as I taught my stuffed animals, my parents knew I would follow in their footsteps and become a teacher. One thing my parents knew is that if I did become a teacher when I grew up, all of my students would have excellent manners, great grades, wonderful conduct, and would not be bullied. This was evidenced by how I turned my loud, rude, lackadaisical group of stuffed animal students into intelligent, sophisticated, and well-behaved individuals.

With the help of my Mom and Dad, I created tests and quizzes for my students, as well as homework assignments. I asked Dad what material he was teaching in class and had him provide an example of an assignment he gave his students. I used this as a resource to map out my own tests and assignments to give my students. Unsurprisingly, my students not only passed, but they did so with flying colors. The class average was a 90, and my students were excelling in reading, writing, and math.

In addition, my parents knew who had gotten in trouble that day at school based on my lesson and reenactment. Of course, my class was better prepared and behaved than people in my physical class at school, but that was because I demanded respect from my students.

I was proud of my students and rewarded them by going outside, which really meant I got to go outside and play. As tough of a teacher as I was, I wished some of that toughness, even a smidgeon, would have transferred to me at school. I should have yelled at the bully who held a fork over me and threatened to stab me, or bit the hand of the bully who dangled me from a two story building, or even slapped the student who slammed me on the hard, tile floor at school. However, there was a big difference between telling a stuffed animal to sit down and be quiet and telling someone two feet taller than me and twice my size to leave me alone.

The positive side is that each obstacle and challenge I experienced made me stronger. I might not have fought back with fists with my bullies, but I fought back with words and education. Being bold in the classroom with my stuffed animals was my escape route, and I prided myself on not giving those who bullied me the satisfaction of seeing me fail.

Chapter 11

Mo' Money Mo' Friends,
No Money No Friends

Every day before I left home for school, my parents gave me lunch money and extra change to get a snack. I began getting creative and thinking outside the box of how to outwit and outsmart my bullies. I was tired of being verbally abused, and I wanted to think of something to save myself from being picked on for at least one day. The idea hit me while I was standing in the snack line in the cafeteria one afternoon.

Lauren, who started bullying me again even after Mom fussed her out, was standing in front of me in the snack line. I shakily and timidly called her name.

"*Lauren*" I said.

She turned around and with an attitude replied, "What?!"

"Would you like me to buy you a snack? I asked shyly.

"Yea, buy me a red fruit roll up."

When I got to the front of the snack line, I said to the cafeteria lady, "May I have one chocolate chip cookie and one red fruit roll up please?"

"Your total is $0.70," the clerk said. I handed her the money, politely said thank you, and got the cookie and fruit roll up.

"Here you go *Lauren*," I said as I handed her the fruit roll up. *Lauren* took it out of my hand, halfheartedly said, "Thanks," and walked off. I was taken aback. For the rest of the day, *Lauren* did not pick on me, make fun of me, or try to snatch the paper off my desk in class. She left me alone, and this was a peculiar feeling because I hardly knew what it felt like to be left alone.

I began using the snack money my parents gave me to buy snacks for the students who bullied me. Before long, word spread like wildfire that I was buying snacks for people, and I was no longer able to accommodate everyone's request. I needed more money because it felt heavenly to go through the day without getting picked on, but how was I going to get the extra money?

I came up with a plan. In the evenings, I walked up to Mom and asked,

"Mom, may I have money for snack?"

She reached into her purse and pulled out $2.

"Here you go" she said.

"Thank you!" I exclaimed.

A few minutes later, I found Dad in his room selecting the suit he was going to wear the next day for work. Double checking and making sure Mom was not in sight, I walked up and asked,

"Dad, may I have money for snack?" He went into his wallet and pulled out $2.

"Here, take this." Dad replied.

"Thank you Dad!" I said as I skipped back to my room.

My plan was successful. I had gotten $4 from my parents, which was enough to buy at least eight snacks for the bullies at school. I felt bad deceiving my parents this way, but I was desperate to get relief from being bullied at school.

For several days, I was able to buy off my bullies. The students who once made fun of me, no longer made fun of my shoes, clothes, hair, or eyes, nor did anyone try to physically bully me. I was safe, at least for a while. However, the good times quickly ended when my parents discovered my technique. Somehow they had figured out that they both had been giving me snack money, and the extra lunch money ended. They also told me that if I tried to deceive them again, I would be in serious trouble.

Another idea came to mind. Dad kept two mason jars full of change in a room in the house. The jar was full of quarters, nickels, dimes, and a few pennies. A thought came to me to take the money out of the jars a little bit at the time. I knew my parents would not suspect anything because the jar was so full of money. They would not miss several quarters here or several dimes there. I knew what I was doing was wrong, but I tried to reassure myself that I would pay back the money eventually. There were a handful of times when I did replace the money, but most of the time, I did not.

With my newfound wealth, I was able to buy snacks for two bullies a day. I never took more than $1.00 out of the change jar, and each snack ranged from

$0.35 to $0.50, so I was covered. For the next few weeks, I bought snacks for two bullies, and these were the two people who bullied me the most. I skipped out on getting myself a snack in order to buy the bully one.

Finally, after about a month, I was fed up and had enough. I started asking myself, *Why should I sacrifice giving up my fruit roll up or chocolate chip cookie for them?* I loved snacks just as much as they did. And, I was taking money from my parents, and that was wrong.

After I made up my mind that the lunch money was mine again, I knew trouble would start. The next day at school, the bullies looked for me to buy them a snack. When I said that I no longer had enough money to buy them a snack, they became furious, and the rude comments commenced again.

"You think you too good to give us your money huh? I should snatch it out yo' hand!" one student said. As I stood in line, a bully flinched at me with her fist balled up as if she were going to hit me. I stepped back in fear and wanted so badly to turn around and sit back down, but I did not want to give her the satisfaction of knowing how scared I really was. If I had walked away, they would have probably made a scene in public, and I did not want to draw more attention to myself than I already had; so I stood there, played with my lunch money, and acted like I did not see or hear them. At this young age, I quickly learned that the more money I had, the more "friends" I had. Yet, "the less money I had, the less "friends" I had.

I not only disliked lunch time because of being bullied out of my money, but I also detested it because I had a hard time fitting in at the lunch table. At lunch, students segregated themselves: black students sat with other black students and white students sat with other white students; there was not much mixing of the races at the different tables. For me, I did not want to sit with people who picked on or made fun of me. I felt more comfortable around my white peers than my black peers, and I sat at the table with white students because they were nicer and more accepting towards me.

One day, a black female student asked me,

"Why you always sit wit dem white people?"

I shrugged my shoulders and said, "I don't know."

She continued and said, "You too good to sit wit us blacks huh? You should sit wit yo' people."

For the first time in a while, a black person welcomed me to their table, and it felt good. I was ecstatic they wanted me to sit with them, but as soon as I sat down, my enthusiasm quickly faded. The students at the table made snide remarks to me, talked about other people, and used profanity. Our table was so loud that my teacher constantly told us to quiet down. When she told us to hush, this only made matters worse, and one student told her,

"Who you think you talking to?" He stood up, got in her face, and said, "I know you ain't talking to me."

He was so blatantly disrespectful, and I knew that was not the table I needed to be sitting. I thought to myself, *Why am I sitting here?*

After the lunch period, my teacher called me aside and said,

"Tensie, why did you sit at that table? You do not act like those students. You are not loud, disrespectful, or rude. You are kind, friendly, and smart. You do not need to hang around them."

With my head held low, I said, "I don't know why I sat there."

She said, "Well, you should go back to sitting at my table. We like when you sit with us."

At that moment, I felt ashamed. I was having a hard time fitting in and was struggling with my identity. I felt like an outcast when I sat with black students, but I liked sitting with my white peers because they treated me nicely and were more accepting of me. After the conversation with my teacher and for the rest of that school year, I sat at the lunch table with my white classmates and felt comfortable. At the table, we talked about important topics, and no one made fun of me or picked on people. I was not attacked, and I felt safe. I began to realize that I identified more with white students than my own race.

Chapter 12

Bullied by a Teacher

Being bullied at school by my peers was a trying experience, but to be bullied by a teacher was an even worse feeling. There is one teacher who bullied me so badly that she greatly affected my self-esteem. Because of her harsh comments and retorts to me in class, to this day, I am still sometimes fearful to speak up in a public setting.

This teacher, who shall remain nameless, was good friends with Mom. I heard so many wonderful things about how well she taught her class and how unique she was, that I was ecstatic when I learned that she would be my fifth grade teacher.

On the first day of school in 1997, I was ready to learn from this great teacher, whom I had heard so much about. My teacher had a unique way of easily alphabetizing students' names by using a number system. She assigned each student a number based on his/her last name. Because my last name started with a "T," my number was 16. Anytime we turned in an assignment, we had to write our first and last name, followed by the number. Each paper I turned in looked like this: Tensie Taylor #16.

The first few weeks of the school year, I loved her class. I stayed after class and helped her by erasing the chalkboard and putting her papers in order. Yet, as time wore on, the happiness I once felt began to fade. I became sad and quiet. I soon learned that my teacher relied heavily on her manuals and did not truly know the subjects she taught. One day, she taught a lesson on conversions.

"How many ounces are in a pound?" she asked.

I raised my hand. She said,

"Yes, Tensie?"

"There are 16 ounces in a pound." I proudly said.

"Wrong! "she replied harshly.

I looked at her in disbelief. I knew I was correct; there were 16 ounces in a pound, and I could not believe she yelled at me in class for giving a right answer. I tried explaining to her that there are 16 ounces in a pound and even pointed to the page of the textbook that said there are 16 ounces in one pound. Her reply was,

"'I'm the teacher, so I should know."

I did not say anything else for the rest of the day.

On another occasion, my teacher spelled words incorrectly. I did not want to embarrass her during class by correcting her, so I waited until after class and told her that she spelled certain words incorrectly. She looked at me and gave me a mean look as if to say, *How dare you try and correct me?* She was insecure and became upset that a ten year old was teaching her things that she, a grown woman, did not know. After this, she started picking on me even more.

One fall afternoon, I was taking extra time to finish an exam. Almost everyone had finished except for a few students. Trying not to rush because I wanted to do well, my thought process was interrupted when she said,

"Tensie, go outside and finish your test in the hallway. I need to move on to a new lesson."

I was surprised by her words and actions because there were other students who were still working on the test, but I was the only one being sent outside in the hallway. Being sent to the hallway was a stigma because only students who misbehaved got sent out in the hallway. As people walked by, students and teachers did a double take.

"Tensie Taylor, what are YOU doing in the hallway?" They asked this question perplexingly because students who sat in the hallway did so for getting in trouble, not for finishing an exam. If a student had to finish a test, the teacher wrote a note and sent him/her to the library or asked the student to go to a classroom close by where a teacher did not have a class at the time. I was embarrassed and worried so much about what people thought in seeing me in the hallway that I quickly rushed through my exam so I could get back to class.

When I walked inside to turn in my exam, my teacher grabbed it, rolled her eyes, and went back to her lesson. "Like I was saying, this…" She treated me as if turning in my exam was bothersome to her.

This teacher who I once loved and admired, I now disliked and detested. I hated her class. When I asked a question, she cut me down and replied in a condescending tone. She found ways to send me to the hallway when I did not do anything at all. One time, I asked her if she could separate my seat from a student who sat close to me and kept talking to me in class because I did not want to get in trouble. The next day when I came into class, she had placed this student's chair directly next to mine.

I became so miserable during class that I began looking at the clock and thinking of increments. "Only two more hours until lunch. Only 30 more minutes until recess. Only 45 minutes left until the bell rings to go home." I studied the clock more than I studied my lesson. It was dreadful, and I was unhappy. I began feeling sick to my stomach whenever I walked into the classroom. I was not myself.

My parents noticed a change in my behavior. The once bubbly girl who ran home to show them what I learned in school that day, the girl who could not stop talking, now was the girl who constantly asked "How many more days until the school year ends?" My passion died because not only was I getting picked on at school by my peers, but my teacher was bullying me, too. I just could not win.

Finally, my parents intervened. Mom tried talking to the teacher since they were good friends, and this only exacerbated matters. My teacher told the guidance counselor at school that Mom fussed her out and yelled at her. The guidance counselor brought Mom and my teacher in for counseling, but after the counseling, it did not help the situation. My teacher and Mom's friendship waned, and my parents began working hard to get me out of her class. Her words, tone, and behavior of singling me out made me feel horrible, and there were days I feigned sickness so I would not have to go to school to face her.

My parents took matters into their own hands, and met with the principal, and asked for me to be taken out of that class. The principal claimed there was nothing she could do and since the school year had started, she did not want to have me switch teachers in the middle of the year. The principal's nonchalance only made my parents madder. Mom and Dad explained to the principal how unhappy I was, how my health was being affected, and how my grades were suffering, but none of that mattered. The principal was too lazy to file the paperwork to get me out of that class. My parents did not give up, and took their frustrations even higher to the school superintendent.

The superintendent listened to the pleas and cries of my parents. Unlike the principal, the superintendent had compassion and empathy, and he instantly asked that I be moved to another teacher's class. The battle that had transpired for weeks was finally over, and we came out victorious. I was immediately moved from that teacher's classroom and placed in another teacher's class who was much more knowledgeable, compassionate and understanding.

After I switched classes, rumors started around school that the only reason I asked to be moved out of the class was because my previous teacher had given me a 'B' in math. I am sure my teacher started this rumor, but I laughed when I heard it because the students did not understand what I had gone through with this teacher. She made my life miserable, and because of how she treated me, she severely lowered my self-esteem.

Because of how curtly this teacher spoke to me in class and demeaned me when I got an answer wrong (when in actuality, I was correct), I became fearful to speak in class. I began to shut down and instead of avidly participating in class, or having the vivacious personality I once did, I became cold and quiet. That teacher negatively affected me and years later, during my time in college, I sometimes hesitated to speak out in class for fear my professors might lash out at me. This was not the case because my professors were great, but it brought back memories to my days in fifth grade when I had this awful, incompetent teacher. Words are powerful, and my teacher tore down my self-esteem, but I kept on pushing.

Chapter 13

Last One Standing

Recess and PE classes were my least favorite areas to participate in during my elementary and middle school years. Recess was supposed to be a fun time, where friends came together, played, and had a good time. There were days—very few—when I had people to play with on the playground. Many times, I was searching to find someone to play with. One day, while I was see-sawing by myself, a classmate came up to me and said,

"I'll get on the see saw with you."

I was taken aback, yet excited because someone wanted to play with me! She was a bigger girl, and she struggled to get on the see-saw, but once she did, we were laughing and having fun going up and down. A few minutes later, I turned my head for a quick second and the see saw slammed to the ground, and I felt pain on my behind. My classmate had gotten off the see-saw, and instead of letting me know and easing down, she jumped off quickly and I came crashing down to the ground. I slowly got up, trying to act like I was not in pain, and went and walked around the playground by myself.

My school had a slide, and I loved sliding. On a warm, spring afternoon, I climbed up the steps and reached the top of the slide and was met by a mean fifth grader. She blocked my way and prevented me from getting onto the slide. I said,

"Excuse me, may I slide?"

She glared at me and said, "No, you too ugly to slide. Get off!"

I turned around and slowly climbed back down the steps. This girl was much bigger than me, and I was not going to argue with her. She would have beaten me to a pulp. What I remember most about her is that although she was in the fifth grade, at 12 years old, she had many missing teeth. She was already too old to be in elementary school because she failed two grades, and her teeth that were missing were permanent. Whenever she smiled, she covered her mouth because she was embarrassed by her teeth. I thought to myself, *The nerve of her to call someone ugly when she has missing teeth*. Her mouth looked like tar because so many of her teeth were rotten and black.

No one ever made fun of her for her teeth. They may have made comments behind her back, but because she was so big, they never said anything to her face. She was a bully, and preyed on small people and from that day on, I never got on the slide again when I saw her on it.

Sometimes during recess, teachers had their classes compete against other classes. We raced, played kickball (which I loved), or played other creative games. When I think back to my elementary school days, kids were not as obese like they are today. This is because we exercised, went outside, and played. Technology was not as popular as it is today. Kids actually did things outside.

When it was time to divide up into two teams, I hated this because I was never chosen as captain of the team. As my classmates eagerly called names to be on teams, I heard some classmates say, "Ooo, pick *James* for our team" or "I would love for *Tammy* to be on our team." When it came to me, I was always the last one picked, and when they called my name, it was as if a judge had sentenced them to life in prison. The grunts, groans, and comments of, "I don't want her on my team" or "She sucks" were all I heard.

One recess period, we participated in a racing game; I was a pretty fast runner. Right before it was my turn to race, I heard someone on my team say,

"Since Tensie has the last leg, I know we're going to lose." Hearing this remark destroyed my confidence, and the vigor and energy I once had, disappeared. When it was my time to run, I did not give it my all. I tried leaning into the finish line to give myself a little leverage to win, but instead I ended up tripping and falling, and skinned my knee badly. The students laughed and thought my injury was so funny. They pointed, and jeers illuminated the outside air. My teacher rushed over to me, told them to stop laughing, and helped me walk to the nurse's office to cover my bruised knee. Not one student tried to help me or asked if I were okay. I believe there were a couple of students who cared because they had concerned looks on their faces, but because they were around their buddies and friends who did not like me, they joined in with the laughter.

To this day, I am not a major fan of basketball. I like to watch this sport, but I do not like to play. My aversion for this sport began when I was in the third grade. During PE class, we were divided into two teams: the red team and the blue team. As expected, I was the last person selected, and I was the shortest person in class. I was placed on the blue team. Picture me, three feet tall, weighing 60 pounds, trying to defend a student who was slightly taller than five feet five inches. It was a struggle.

Everything I learned, I took seriously. My parents taught me that if I learned something, whether it was for academics or athletics, I needed to perform it well. We had a basketball goal in my parents' yard, and each night, I worked on my dribbling and shooting free throws. Some nights, I did not go inside until I made 100 free throws. I was determined to become better in basketball in hopes students would not tease me at school.

As much as I practiced at home, when I got in class, all my skills and techniques went out the window. As we played a game during PE class, I kept extending my arms in the air, begging my teammates to pass me the ball. Each person on my team passed it to other teammates, except me. When I said, "Come on, pass it here." They laughed and passed it over my head to another teammate. I jumped as high as I could and tried to catch the ball they threw to someone else, but I was not successful.

My PE teacher sensed my frustration and noticed that students were not including me in the game, so she blew her whistle and stopped the game. She said,

"Everyone needs to play fairly. I noticed that no one has passed the ball to Tensie. If y'all don't pass her the ball, we'll pack up right now and you'll go back to class."

The teacher stood up for me, and I knew I would now have a chance to play. The students, however, were upset at the possibility of having to end recess early because of me, so they did throw me the ball, but they did it harshly. One student threw the ball so hard to me that it hit my chest and slipped out my hand and the other team got it and scored. Now, my teammates really hated me and picked on me even harder. In one instance when the teacher was not looking, a student threw the ball and hit me in the back of the head.

"You don't know how to play anything." They taunted.

I tried to redeem myself by showing them that I did have a few basketball skills. I decided to make a shot. This shot, ended up being like the shot Carlton Banks made in season 1 episode 11 of the Fresh Prince of Bel Air when he stole the ball from Will. That ball went in the air and came nowhere near the goal. Where I was shooting, no one will ever know, and my shot was way worse than an air ball. My classmates laughed and picked at me even more, and at this point, I loathed basketball.

We finished the basketball game, and my team lost. My teammates said that we lost because of me. I do know one thing for sure: I may have been the last one standing in sports, but I was definitely not the last one standing in academics.

2001: My brother Jemonde and I playing trumpet
together at Christmas Eve service in Louisburg, NC

1989: My sister Kelise (l), brother Jemonde (center),
and I (r) all playing together at my parents' home

2009: (left to right) Mom, me, Dad, my brother Jemonde, and sister Kelise worshipping at Hickory Grove Baptist Church in Louisburg, NC

2008: Myself with my scholarship donor, Mrs. Jean F. Gilmore, at the CHASS Scholarship Banquet at North Carolina State University in Raleigh, NC

2004: Kissing the Blarney Stone in Ireland.

2004: Visiting Stonehenge in London, England at
16 years old

2004: Playing piano in Westminster Cathedral Hall in
London, England for Queen Elizabeth's knight, Sir
Andrew

2002: (left to right) Aunt Tent, my cousin Lisa, me, Mom, and Dad at Stanford University for my brother Jemonde's graduation

2005: (left to right) Dad, my high school guidance counselor Cherry Ayscue, and I after I won first place in the Veterans of Foreign Wars essay contest

2005: My senior high school graduation picture from Louisburg High School

2002: Speaking at Louisburg College at the MLK Banquet. Governor of North Carolina Beverly Perdue looks on

2004: My brother Jemonde and I at my parents' home
in Louisburg, NC

2001: My Mom and I at a banquet I was honored at in
Winston-Salem, NC

2000: My family and I on vacation at Wrightsville Beach, NC

2000: Cheerleader at Terrell Lane Middle School, 8th grade

2000: Myself with my classmates after we performed *How the Grinch Stole Christmas* at Terrell Lane Middle School. I was Little Cindy Lou Who

1997: Anchoring the news at 10 years old with WRAL news anchor Debra Morgan

1990: Myself at three years old

1995: Myself with actress Tonea Stewart from the show
In The Heat of the Night

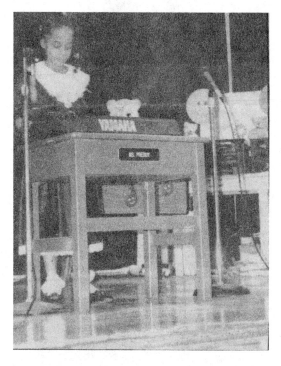

1997: Playing the keyboard at an elementary school after reciting Dr. King's *I Have a Dream* speech at an assembly program

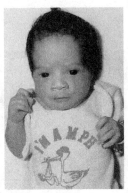

Myself at birth, August 1987

Myself on the first day of Kindergarten, 1992

Myself with Mrs. Privette after I graduated from St. Paul's Day Care Center in 1991

2015: Myself with Beyonce's Mom, Tina Lawson, at the Reed for Hope Fundraiser

2015: Interviewing singer Eric Benet on the red carpet in Beverly Hills, CA

2014: Interviewing actor Aaron Spears from *Being Mary Jane* at the NAACP Theater Awards at the Saban Theatre

2014: Interviewing actress Kathy Bates at the Ninth Annual Evening under the Stars at Sony Pictures Studios

2014: With singer and actress Brandy at the 2014
Hollywood Confidential

2014: Graduating with my Master's Degree in Postsecondary Administration and Student Affairs from the University of Southern California's Rossier School of Education

2009: Graduating with my Bachelor's Degree in
Communication – Media, minor in Psychology from
North Carolina State University's College of
Humanities and Social Sciences

Mom and Dad with actors/models Boris Kodjoe and
Nicole Ari Parker at a private gala in California in 2015

2015: Honored alongside Boris Kodjoe at the Millennium Momentum Foundation's Opening Doors Gala at the Dorothy Chandler Pavilion, former home of the Oscars, in downtown Los Angeles

May 2014: Celebrating my graduation from the
University of Southern California where I received my
Master's in Education with my family (left to right)
brother Jemonde, Dad, Mom, me, Uncle Thomas,
cousin Michael, cousin Jarrett

March 2014: Alternative Spring Break trip to
Guatemala, where we, USC students, built an office for
a principal at an elementary school.

1995: Autographed picture from renowned lawyer
Willie Gary given to me after he heard me recite at an
MLK Banquet in North Carolina

1994: 1st grade when I read 108 books in Mrs.
Harrison's class. The books I read ranged from 100-600
pages. I received a trophy, plaque, and shirt.

1995 Autographed picture from actress Tonea Stewart
given to me after she heard me recite at an MLK
Banquet in North Carolina

1997: Autographed picture from news anchor Debra
Morgan after I anchored the news for a day on WB 50

2001: My sister Kelise and I with Chelsea Clinton at Stanford University's bookstore

2015: Received camera time on The Ellen Show

Chapter 14
Dreading Awards Day

Receiving an award should be a happy and joyous occasion. All of the hard work, time, effort, and energy a person puts into perfecting an assignment and then being rewarded for it would make anyone smile. Unfortunately, this was not how I felt. Every single year, I dreaded awards day. Why? Because my classmates said negative remarks each time I was called on stage to receive an award. I detested awards day because even though I worked hard for the school year and was proud of my academic accomplishments, I knew I was going to get tormented and verbally bullied on that day. The silver lining was counting on the support of Mom, Dad, Jemonde, and Kelise to clap and cheer for me when my name was called. To see their smiling faces in the crowd made me feel better.

As the award's ceremony began, teachers read criteria for the awards, and then called students' names.

"For highest average in mathematics…Tensie Taylor."

I walked to the stage, accepted my award, shook the teacher's hand, said thank you, and then took my seat.

"For reading 108 books this year…Tensie Taylor."

By the second time, this is where the grunts and groans of my classmates began.

"For the highest average in language arts...Tensie Taylor." As I walked up to the stage, students smirked,

"I am so sick of her. She wins everything and won't give anyone else a chance to win."

"For 1st place winner in the oratorical contest...Tensie Taylor."

As I walked up to the stage, I heard students smacking their lips and groaning because my name was being called again. By this time, their taunts started to affect my confidence, and as more awards were being presented, I prayed that my name was not called.

"For first place winner in the Veteran of Foreign Wars' essay contest...Tensie Taylor"

"For perfect attendance...Tensie Taylor."

"For first place winner in the spelling bee...Tensie Taylor."

"For 1st place winner in the Soil & Water Conservation essay contest...Tensie Taylor."

This time, as I got up, one student stuck out her leg and tried to trip me. Fortunately, I noticed her action and stepped over her leg. As the awards kept rolling in, all I heard was,

"She is such a teacher's pet."

"She has no life because all she does is study."

"You know her parents won't let her watch TV or have any fun right? All she does is read and do homework. They won't let her go nowhere."

"I could win an award if she didn't take everything from everybody." Students remarked.

The commentary was taking its toll on me, and I was sinking deeper and deeper into sadness. I even began to slouch with my posture because I felt ashamed from their comments.

When one student received the most improved award, my classmates erupted in applause, stood up, screamed, and cheered loudly. This was the only award she received, and the classmates gave her a standing ovation. But when I received several awards, all I received were jeers and negative commentary. The awardee walked by me and said,

"See, you don't win everything."

There was another program at school called the Accelerated Reader Program, where students read books, took a test, and depending on the grade level of the book, received a certain amount of points for each book read. I have loved reading since I was in kindergarten. I read books that were 100 to 600 pages, including fiction, non-fiction, biographies, comedies, suspense, drama, anything I picked up, I read.

My mother, the Librarian at my school, awarded students who were 1st, 2nd, and 3rd place winners with prizes. Each month, Mom announced over the intercom,

"Good Morning boys and girls. It's that time again! Accelerated reader time!"

Students in my class laughed because of the greeting Mom gave. Students commented,

"Well we know who's going to win 1st place again...Tensie." I held my head in shame because I knew I would be the first place winner and students would make snide remarks. Over the intercom, Mom continued,

"1st place, Tensie Taylor with 105.7 points." Instead of congratulating me, a student remarked,

"The only reason you keep winning is because your Mom is in charge of the program. She probably cheats for you. I'll be glad when she's gone so you won't win everything."

I pretended I was working on an assignment and ignored her. I knew the truth, and Mom never cheated for me; I worked hard to earn those points, read those books, and took the tests. I desperately wanted a student to congratulate me, to say something positive, but instead, it was either a negative remark, a smack of the lips, an eye roll, or the phrase, "I'm sick of her." I did not work hard in school to receive gratitude and praise from my peers, but it would have been nice to have a few of my classmates say, "Good job Tensie." Unfortunately, that did not happen often.

After an award's day ceremony in fifth grade, I was proud of myself. I received several plaques, medallions, certificates, and trophies for my academic merit. I had so many awards that my teacher helped me carry them back to the classroom. I placed some awards on the desk and others on the floor. One particular student came by and knocked two of my trophies from my desk onto the floor and another student kicked several trophies on the floor. I looked at them in bemusement with hurt in my eyes. They retorted,

"Just because you won all these awards don't mean you gonna be successful in life. Yo' Mom helped you get those awards and when she don't work here no mo', you won't get no mo' awards. You ain't as smart as you think you is."

With a broken heart and listening to their bad, broken English, I held my head low and kneeled down to pick up my trophies off the floor. My moment of euphoria and pride for myself quickly faded. If students did not want to congratulate me or did not like me, that was fine, but why did they have to go out of their way to make cruel comments?

When the school day ended, Mom came and helped me put my trophies in the car. "I am so incredibly proud of you Janine! You won so many awards! All of your hard work paid off and it will continue to pay off!"

"Thanks," I say faintly."

"What's wrong?" Mom asked.

As I told her what happened, she said,

"Pay those students no mind. Always remember this: the same people who pick on you now are going to be the same people asking for your help later in life. Keep working hard and persevering. I know it's difficult, but ignore them. They are just jealous."

Once we got home, I got out the car and gave her a great big bear hug and said, "Thank you Mom!" Mom's words echoed in my ear that day, and they still echo with me today. As I continued to be bullied at school and people made snarky and snide remarks, I tried my best to ignore them. I kept my goals, dreams, aspirations, and the big picture in my mind at all times.

Chapter 15

Would I Ever Be Queen

I was not treated like a queen or princess at school, but I was fortunate and blessed to be treated like a princess at home by my Dad and brother Jemonde. Each morning from primary to high school, Dad fixed breakfast for me. When I say breakfast, I am not referring to half a banana, a grape, and a glass of water. Dad cooked a variety of foods and fixed a delicious, southern breakfast that consisted of grits, eggs, sausage, toast, pancakes, waffles, French toast, bacon, applesauce, oatmeal, Toaster strudel, apple juice, or orange juice. I enjoyed waking up each morning and going to the kitchen table to see what meal Dad had prepared. He was a chef!

On weekends, Jemonde cooked fancy breakfasts, such as delicious crepes with powdered sugar. He cooked various cuisines, ranging from Spanish food to Ethiopian to French food. My mouth watered when I smelled his meal in the kitchen, and I could not wait to eat! Mom cooked too, and is known for her delicious cakes, pies, banana pudding, yams, casserole, beef stew, anything and everything one can think of, she makes.

What I loved most about my family's cooking was that they always made a baby portion for me. If Mom or Jemonde fixed pancakes, they made a baby pancake for me that was about the size of my hand. When Dad made sausage, he made a baby sausage for me. They liked picking on me, and I thought it was cute to have a smaller portion. Every time dinner was served, and there was steak, a hamburger patty, or a biscuit, everyone knew which portion was mine.

Dad not only fixed me breakfast every morning, but in the late fall and winter months, he started my Mom's car and when I got my license, he started my car, too. He went outside in the cold, started the car, turned on the heat and defrost, and let the car run for several minutes. By the time Mom and I left for work and school, the car was warm and toasty. I did not have to sit in my car like an eskimo waiting for it to warm up; I simply hopped in and enjoyed the warmth. I was snug as a bug.

While I was being treated like royalty at home, I was treated like a peasant by students at school. One event I desperately wanted to be a part of was the Homecoming court. I wanted to either be a princess or Homecoming Queen. My siblings had both been on the court, and I saw how beautiful and handsome they looked, and I, too wanted to be a part of it.

To be on the Homecoming court, students in each grade voted. The choices were freshman princess, sophomore princess, junior princess, and Homecoming queen (typically given to a senior). During my freshman year, I did a double take and saw my name on the ballot. I was shocked because I did not think I was popular enough for my name to be on there. I remember coming home and screaming to my parents,

"I made it as freshman princess on the Homecoming ballot!"

Mom and Dad exclaimed, "You did? That's wonderful! I know how much this means to you! I hope you get it!"

As badly as I wanted to be on the Homecoming court, I knew in my heart I would not be chosen. Because I was bullied at school so much and people thought of me as a geek and nerd, I knew they did not like me enough to vote for me.

I remember sitting in my homeroom class at Louisburg High School, anticipating the results.

"Thank you for listening to today's announcements. The votes are in, and freshman princess is..." I held my breath in anticipation,

"*Kylie!*" the announcer exclaimed. My classmates erupted in applause. I was very disappointed, and did not listen to the rest of the announcements to see who else was on the court. Although I was disappointed, I was not a sore loser, and I congratulated *Kylie* for winning freshman princess. She said thank you and continued celebrating with her friends in the corner.

I later learned from a teacher who counted the ballots that I was one vote away from making it onto the Homecoming court. As upset as I was, I found the positivity in the situation, knowing I had three more years to try and get on the Homecoming court. I was determined.

Before I knew it, sophomore year rolled around, and it was time for Homecoming again. I erased what happened the year before and looked forward to a better year. When we went into our homeroom class, I noticed that my name was not listed on the ballot. Yet, there was still hope. My school allowed students to write in a name if it was not listed. It could either be our name or another student's name. I decided to write in my name and to increase my chances, I asked several students if they could write in my name on the ballot. I shared with them that it was a dream of mine to be on the court. Some students looked at me in disgust and laughed,

"Do you really think I would write in your name? You gotta be kidding me"

Discouraged again, I turned in my ballot and wished that I would be selected. Several days later after all ballots had been counted, I listened attentively to the afternoon announcements.

"Thank you for listening to today's announcements. The votes are in, and sophomore princess is *Kelly!*" the announcer said.

Realizing my name was not called, I was hurt again, but I showed good sportsmanship and congratulated *Kelly* later that day when I saw her in the hallway. All hope was not lost because I had another idea. I learned that a guy who liked me had been selected as one of the princes on the court. Because I so badly wanted to be on the Homecoming court, I asked him if he had someone in mind to escort. He did. My face perked up because I was hoping he would say my name.

"My escort will be my cousin." He said.

I had to make sure I heard him right.

"What?" I asked surprisingly.

"I'm escorting my cousin. Look, I know you know I like you and all, but I don't want other people to know I like you." And he walked off.

I stood there in shock at what I heard. He would escort his cousin, even though he liked me, because he didn't want people to find out that he liked me. That made absolutely no sense. Instead of him seeing it as a positive of escorting the girl he liked, he saw it as an embarrassment for him to be seen with me. Guys.

The reason I wanted to be on the Homecoming court was because it showed popularity. People knew my name, but only because of academics. I wanted to be known as someone other than "Oh, Tensie's she's smart." I wanted to be seen as popular or someone with style and sophistication. Furthermore, I absolutely loved shopping for evening gowns and getting my hair, nails, and makeup done. Many students on the Homecoming court were popular, and I wanted to be a part of that circle, too. I convinced myself that if I made it onto the court, people would no longer see me as a geek or teacher's pet, but as a cool person. I also thought that if I made the court, this might deter the bullying I faced at school. I would no longer have to hear people make fun of me or worry about them throwing food at me in the cafeteria. I would not be a dweeb.

My junior year of high school came, and I was optimistic yet again about being on the Homecoming court. When we received the ballot in homeroom, I was shocked to see my name on there. I felt pumped! I drifted off with my thoughts and pictured myself dress shopping with Mom, looking through magazines to find the right hairstyle, practicing my smile in the mirror for pictures, and holding back the tears when the tiara was placed on my head. Mom told me things happened in threes, and since I had been rejected twice, this must be lucky number three. I checked my name on the ballot and checked a few other students' names, and turned my ballot in smiling.

Several days later during the afternoon announcements, I heard,

"The following ladies will be on the Homecoming court." The announcer said over the intercom. My heart was pounding, but in a good way because I felt confident my name would be called.

"Congratulations to *Kelsey*, *Terry*, and *Shonda* who are our freshman, sophomore, and junior princesses."

As Langston Hughes poetically once wrote, "a dream deferred." My dream of being on the Homecoming court was deferred and this time, three was not a lucky number. I struck out three times, and I felt more and more defeated. I did not have the energy to congratulate the winners; I was sulking in my despair.

Yet, for every negative in the situation, I saw the positive. For the second time, my name made it onto the ballot, and I did not have to worry about a guy dissing me. In the words of Jesse Jackson at his 1988 Democratic National Convention Address, "Keep hope alive!" I heeded these words and kept hoping that for my senior year, I would finally make it onto the Homecoming court.

In October 2004, my senior year rolled around, and I reached this year with anticipation. It was my last year of high school, and I looked forward to starting the college application process. But before that, I was nervously excited about the outcome of the Homecoming court. This was my last and final year to make my dream of being on the court a reality. I reflected on the past three years: freshman year: my name made it onto the ballot, but I did not make the court; sophomore year: I was laughed at and dissed; junior year: I made it onto the ballot again, but did not win, and this year, I planned to walk the court. This was my year! I just knew it. I went to homeroom and filled out my final ballot. I smiled because I saw my name on there and thought this was a good sign. I checked my name, circled a few other names, and happily turned in my ballot.

Several days later, the afternoon announcements came on and the votes were in.

"Good afternoon teachers and students. These are your announcements."

She began announcing upcoming events and after what seemed like an eternity, she finally began announcing those who made it onto the Homecoming court. I waited in anticipation as she called those who made the court for freshmen, sophomore, and junior princesses and princes.

"The following seniors have made the Homecoming Court" the announcer said.

I closed my eyes, crossed my fingers, and relentlessly said to myself *please let me get chosen.*

I listened attentively to the names called, and unfortunately, my name was not one of them. Slowly and sadly, I opened my eyes and held my head down, trying not to cry. For four years, I diligently tried to make it onto the Homecoming court, and now my time had come to an end. Why didn't people like me? Why was I not chosen when it came to popularity contests? I had no problem getting selected to be class president, but when it came to something social, I was never chosen. I asked myself numerous *why* questions until I heard the bell ring to dismiss us from school. All I wanted to do was go home and cry. I did not congratulate those who had been selected, not to be spiteful, but because I genuinely did not want to.

After wallowing in my misery and having a pity party for a couple of days, I decided to bring back my positive energy. Even though I could not walk the Homecoming court, I could be my own queen and treat myself to a day of pampering. Everything I dreamed about doing before Homecoming, I could still do. I could get my hair and nails done. I did not need my classmates' votes for me to feel beautiful; I could treat myself and make me feel beautiful.

On the day of Homecoming, I received permission to leave school early. We had a pep rally that afternoon, so I did not miss any classes or school work.

My hairstylist worked at JC Penny in Henderson, North Carolina. She styled my hair the year before for my junior prom, and I received many compliments. I brought in a picture to show her how I wanted my hair. She was very talented, and I knew she would hook me up.

While sitting in her chair, I carried on a conversation with her. She asked me if I had a special occasion I was attending. I replied, "Yes. Tonight is Homecoming, and I want to look pretty!"

"Are you going to be on the Homecoming court?" she inquired.

I was still licking my wounds from not being selected, but I cleared my throat and said,

"No ma'am, but I am celebrating in spirit and want to look good!" I exclaimed.

"Good for you!" she said, as she shampooed my hair. She shampooed, conditioned, blow dried, and styled my hair. After she finished, I looked in the mirror and saw how absolutely gorgeous it was! She styled it into an up do with a simple and elegant design. I admired my hair from the front, back, right and left sides. I loved it.

"Thank you, thank you, thank you! Tonight is going to be lovely!" I shouted.

I paid her, gave her a nice tip, and walked out of the salon feeling lovely. I left the hair salon and headed to the nail salon to get a French manicure. I was determined to have a classy and enchanted evening at Homecoming.

Following my afternoon of beauty, I returned home. As soon as I walked into the house, Mom said,

"My, My, My, don't you look nice! Your hair is pretty."

I replied, "Thank you Mom!"

I headed to my room to begin getting ready for the evening. I wanted to wear a cute, classy outfit, but because I was in the marching band, I had to wear the band attire: Khaki pants with a light blue shirt. It was October and the weather was chilly, so I also wore my blue and orange band jacket. Blue and orange were Louisburg High School's colors and our mascot was the Warrior. There was not much I could do to make this outfit cute, but at least with my hairdo, nails, and makeup, I could still look pretty.

I sat in the chair in my room and began applying my makeup. I put on honey-colored foundation, held my jaws in like a fish and applied my rosy blush, opened my eyes to apply mascara, and pursed my lips to put the finishing touches on my pink lip color. Next, I found a nice pair of gold earrings to complete my look. I looked at myself in the mirror and loved what I saw. I still struggled with the size of my eyes, but for the most part, I thought I looked pretty. I grabbed my not so cute jacket, picked up my trumpet and sheet music, got in my car and drove to school to play for Homecoming.

When I reached Louisburg High School, I parked my car, gathered my belongings, and walked towards the band room. A few people were hanging on the steps outside, and said,

"I like your hair Tensie!"

I smiled and said, "Thank you so much," and walked inside.

Hearing that compliment made me feel good, and I was happy. I began getting excited about Homecoming, even though I was not on the Homecoming court. I was going to enjoy myself and have a fun and eventful night. As the night wore on, my confidence and excitement waned. After unpacking my trumpet, I began doing the warm up exercises, Remington, which consisted of going up and down the scales to warm up my lips. By this time, a group of students, who I was not particularly fond of, walked in. These girls constantly had something to say about people, especially me. I tried to ignore this clique and continued warming up as they walked by. They did not say anything to me as they passed, but once they took their seats, they kept staring at me. After staring at me, they looked at each other, whispered something, and then looked back at me and laughed. I knew they were talking about me.

By this time, I began feeling warm and embarrassed. The confidence I once exuded was gone. Other students started to arrive and began warming up, too. As I was warming up, one girl stood up and said,

"Hey Tensie, why you got yo hair done for? You tryna be cute? It looks ugly."

At that moment, she and her clique started laughing. I tried to ignore them and continued playing my trumpet, but her words bothered me. I was still discouraged from not being chosen for the Homecoming court, and I had cheered myself up by having a day of beauty. Within minutes, my self-esteem came crashing down again, and I became angry at myself. Instead of being mad at the girls who were making fun of me, I became mad at myself. Why did I decide to get my hair done? Why did I waste money on getting a French manicure? It was dumb of me to get dolled up for an evening that I had no part in. I set myself up for this ridicule and torment, or so I thought.

That night, I hated Homecoming. I was bitter that my peers did not vote for me to make it onto the court in four years. I was mad that the girls were making fun of me. And I was furious at myself for looking like a complete idiot with my hair, nails, and makeup done, when the only way people saw me on the court was playing my trumpet.

For the rest of the evening, I put on a façade and did everything in my power not to cry. Paul Laurence Dunbar wrote a poem entitled, *We Wear the Mask*, and this poem described how I felt that night, as well as many other times in life:

> We wear the mask that grins and lies,
> It hides our cheeks and shades our eyes,
> This debt we pay to human guile;
> With torn and bleeding hearts we smile,
> And mouth with myriad subtleties.
>
> Why should the world be over-wise,
> In counting all our tears and sighs?
> Nay, let them only see us, while
> We wear the mask.
>
> We smile, but, O great Christ, our cries
> To thee from tortured souls arise.
> We sing, but oh the clay is vile
> Beneath our feet, and long the mile;
> But let the world dream otherwise,
> We wear the mask!

I wore the mask that night and many other times throughout my life. I did not understand why students were so juvenile, mean, and malicious. To demean others was such childish behavior and showed just how insecure a person was. If the girls did not like my hair, so what? Why did they feel the need to belittle me when

I had done nothing to them? If the tables were turned and I picked on them for their low grades and poor hygiene, the students would be ready to fight me. I refused to stoop to their level. My parents also taught me to never make fun of or demean other people. Perhaps, the parents of the students who bullied me did not teach their children manners or respect.

The good news is that I made it through Homecoming, and even though I was never voted princess or Homecoming Queen, I was treated like royalty at home, and that's all that really mattered.

Chapter 16

Sleepovers Almost Turned Deadly

My parents were never fond of me sleeping over at a friend's house. There were three times in my life when I spent the night at a friend's house, two of those times being horrible experiences. On one occasion, I spent a night at *Janice's* house, and the slumber party almost ended in tragedy. After much begging and pleading with my parents, Mom and Dad agreed to let me stay with *Janice*. Mom dropped me off at her house, and the fun commenced. We played outside, rode with her parents to lunch, went to the movies, and concluded with dinner and television night at her parents' home.

"Time for bed," *Janice's* Mom said. I took my bath first and put on my pajamas and *Janice* took her bath next. We were all fresh and clean and ready to drift into a peaceful slumber.

"Don't forget to say your prayers." *Janice's* Mom said. *Janice* and I kneeled by the bed and in unison said,

Now I lay me down to sleep,
I pray to the Lord my soul to keep.
If I should die before I wake,
I pray to the Lord my soul to take. Amen.'

"Goodnight Tensie," *Janice* said.

"Goodnight *Janice*." I replied. "Sleep tight and don't let the bedbugs bite." Mom taught me this saying, and I used it regularly.

After having such a fun and energetic day, I found it difficult to drift off to sleep, so I stared at the ceiling, trying to make myself sleepy. *Janice* was afraid of the dark, so she had on her night light. As I continued staring at the ceiling and started counting in my head, my eyelids became heavier and heavier, and I finally drifted off to sleep.

I was not sure how long the time had passed, but the next thing I knew, I woke up to a pillow over my face with *Janice* trying to smother me. Panicked and terribly afraid, I began kicking and screaming, but *Janice's* parents did not hear my cries because the pillow was muffling my sound. With my arms flailing and fighting for my life, I somehow maneuvered and wiggled myself out of *Janice's* hold. When I jerked up, I was gasping for air, coughing, and looking at my friend in utter disbelief and shock. What exactly was she trying to do? Was she trying to kill me?

"What in the world is wrong with you *Janice*?" I snapped.

"You betta not tell on me or I might just finish you off." She laughed evilly and gave me a demonic look before she pulled the covers over her head and went back to bed.

I was incredibly terrified to get back in the bed because I feared for my life. I was too scared to tell *Janice's* parents for fear of what might happen next. I sat next to the bedroom door and fearfully stayed awake all night until I saw the sun begin to rise. I felt safer being near the door in case *Janice* tried to harm me again. It was miserable waiting, but I was not sure what else I could do. At that moment, all I wanted was to be at home, safe and sound in the comfort of my own bed. It was then and there that I understood why my parents were so hesitant about me spending the night at friends' houses. Anything could happen, including my being killed.

The next day, I hurriedly put my clothes on and asked *Janice's* Mom if she could take me home immediately. *Janice* was still asleep and stayed with her Dad, while her Mom took me home.

When we got in the car, *Janice's* Mom asked,

"Is something wrong? You seem in a hurry to leave."

Janice's words echoed in my mind: *You better not tell on me or I might just finish you off.* I was afraid to tell, but I knew I had to. This girl tried to smother me to death, and her mother had a right to know.

"I had a very bad night last night. I was asleep in bed and the next thing I know, your daughter, *Janice,* tried to smother me with a pillow. I began kicking and screaming, but I don't believe you heard me because the pillow stifled my sound. After wiggling out, I was able to free myself, and *Janice* threatened to finish me off if I told you. I have never been so scared in my life."

As I recounted the events of the previous night, my voice was shaky, my hands were trembling, and I was sweating profusely. I was worried about what would happen next.

"Are you serious?" *Janice's* Mom asked. "I am sorry that happened to you. I wish you would have told me last night. No need to worry, *Janice* will be punished."

At that moment, we pulled up to my parents' house and got out of the car. I told Mom and Dad what happened and again *Janice's* Mom apologized profusely, and said,

"Rest assured, *Janice* will be dealt with."

After that incident, I looked at *Janice* so differently, and I never felt safe visiting her again. I did not spend a night at her house again because of the traumatic experience I went through. For days and weeks following that incident, I continued to relive what transpired. I could not believe I went to a friend's house expecting to have a fun sleepover, and almost ended up dying. I wondered if *Janice* purposefully invited me over to her house to harm me. I never said much to her after that incident, and each night when I said my prayers, the words, *if I should die before I awake,* rang through my ears, and it hit me that I could have died that night. I thank God I was able to maneuver my way out, and I still do not know how I escaped. It was probably one of God's angels who protected me.

***

A few years later, I was excited when a student named *Karina*, asked if I wanted to spend a night at her house with other friends for her birthday. As soon as she asked me this question, my mind flashed back to the last time I spent the night at a friend's house and almost died. However, I wanted to fit in and this girl was popular, and I felt special that she asked me to attend. I desperately wanted to be liked, so I asked my parents if I could go. Mom and Dad were even more hesitant about me going because of what happened the last time at a sleepover. But because Mom knew *Karina's* mother, Mom felt it would be okay, and she and Dad gave me permission to go.

The Saturday of that week, Dad drove me to *Karina's* house and dropped me off. He met her Mom and told me he would be back the next morning to pick me up. I went inside, and met *Karina's* other friends, some who I knew. We did not have the same circle of friends, and the other friends who were invited were troublemakers.

As the slumber party commenced, I realized how out of place I felt. I did not listen to the same music as *Karina* and her friends, they used profanity, and they were making plans to retaliate on a girl they did not like. This made me nervous, and my thoughts were interrupted when *Karina* said,

"Come on y'all, get in the car. We goin' to her house. We'll show her. Aye! Grab that butcher knife and let's go."

I was so stricken with fear I could hardly move. *Karina's* Mom had left, so we were on our own. The words, *go to her house* and *get that butcher knife* terrified me, and I did not want to be a part of this slumber party anymore. I began to get angry at myself. Why in the world did I put myself through this again by spending the night at someone else's house? Had I not learned my lesson the first time? I quickly tried to think of an excuse to call home. Maybe I could say I wasn't feeling well or that my period came on. Something, anything, to get out of there. Sadly, as scared as I was, I did not want to look like a punk and wanted to fit in with this girl, so I calmed myself down and hopped in the car with them, and rode along to the girl's house.

When we got in the car, *Karina* turned up the radio, and everyone, except me, was dancing and laughing. In between songs on the radio, *Karina* made threatening calls to the girl's house. I quietly sat in the back seat with knots in my stomach fearing for my life. I tried to fake laugh at times to fit in, but I was deathly afraid. I said a silent prayer and asked God to please watch over me.

By this time, night had fallen, and *Karina* was close to the girl's house. She did not pull up directly to her house, but parked a few blocks down the street because she wanted to surprise her, and not in a good way. The area the girl lived in was not very nice or safe. My heart was beating out of my chest because I was so scared.

"Alright y'all, get out. Let's go inside and jump her!" *Karina* said. She reached down under the seat and pulled out the butcher knife, opened the door, and got out the car. The other two girls got out, but I softly said, "Y'all go ahead. I'll stay in the car."

Karina said, "What? You scared?" You a lil' punk.

The girls began walking to the house, and I crouched down in the backseat. *Karina* had taken the keys, so there was nowhere for me to go if something happened. I was tremendously afraid, and I tried not to cry. I prayed instead, *Please God. Please please please God. Protect me and get me out of here. If You get me out of this situation, I will never spend another night at a friend's house again.*

After what seemed like an eternity, *Karina* and her friends came back to the car.

"Why you all crouched down on the floor?" *Karina* asked. "You really are scared huh? Awww, Tensie's scared."

Everyone started laughing as they got back in the car. I did not want to go to jail; I did not want to be involved with this. One bad thing could happen, and my future or life could be ruined.

I heard *Karina* say, "Let's go home y'all. Tensie's scared." I later learned that after knocking and kicking the door, the girl they were trying to jump never let them inside. Thank God because if she had, who knows what would have happened? With the butcher knife and as mad as *Karina* and her friends were, someone might have been killed.

We got back to the house, and *Karina's* Mom was there.

"Where have y'all been?" she asked.

"Oh, we just went riding." *Karina* said.

That night, I do not know if I slept. I was waiting for morning so I could call Dad and tell him to pick me up. The next morning, I did just that, and Dad came and picked me up. I said goodbye to *Karina,* her Mom, and friends, and hurriedly left.

"How was the sleep over?" Dad asked.

"It was fine." I said shortly. For the rest of the trip home, I rode in silence and thanked God for not allowing anything bad to happen. I did not tell my parents what happened because I did not want to scare them, nor did I want them to mention anything to *Karina's* Mom. I was simply thankful that the Good Lord had watched over me, yet again.

That Monday at school, I heard that *Karina* had gone over to the girl's house again, gotten into a fight, and the police were called. I felt relieved that I was not mixed up in that mayhem. For the rest of my school year until I graduated from high school, I never spent a night at anyone's house again. I valued my life and the fact that God had spared me twice from being harmed or killed, I decided not to press my luck any further.

Chapter 17

Sexually Assaulted at 14

It was the summer of 2002, and my family flew to California to celebrate my brother's graduation from Stanford University. He received a Master of Science in Mechanical Engineering, and we were extremely proud of his accomplishments. We had a lovely time, and not only were we there to celebrate this magnificent milestone in his life, but we were there to also enjoy California! We toured Stanford University's campus, visited the Golden Gate Bridge, got locked up in jail at Alcatraz (for pretend, of course), drove down Lombard Street, and took hundreds of pictures. We ate clam chowder in a bread bowl at Fisherman's Warf and enjoyed the gorgeous lights from the San Francisco-Oakland Bay Bridge.

After spending several days in San Francisco, we headed to Los Angeles. This is where I fell in love with the city of angels! Because of the gorgeous rays of sunshine, the beautiful beaches, the diverse population of people, and the delicious food, I was easily sold and determined to live in this great city one day!

Early that afternoon, my family decided to go to Universal Studios. We rode several rides, took a tour that showed us how movies were made, ate yummy food, and had a blast. As we walked through the theme park, one attraction caught my eye: Jurassic Park! Jurassic Park was one of my favorite movies as a child, and I immediately ran up to the dinosaur and asked Jemonde to take a picture of me. He obliged.

"Come on! Come on! Let's ride!" I pleaded. My parents had enough entertainment for the day, so my brother went with me on the ride. The ride was a water ride and had a big drop at the end, and Mom was not too fond of going down big drops because she got butterflies in her stomach.

"Let's go Janine." Jemonde exclaimed, as I happily skipped in line. Being my talkative self, Jemonde and I talked as we waited in line. It took about 25 minutes until it was our time to hop in the Jurassic Park ride! When it was time to get on the ride, the seat was long enough to seat three people. Normally, I sat next to Jemonde on rides so I could be close to him in case something happened, but this time, for whatever reason, that did not happen. Instead, a white guy—who was a solo rider—went first, and I followed and sat next to him, and then Jemonde sat on the end. We were not thinking, but Jemonde should have switched places and been in the middle, instead of me. Nonetheless, I was too excited to be on this ride and never would have imagined what would happen next.

The white guy smiled and spoke to me,

"Hi!" Because my big, brother was to the right of me, I felt protected and safe and politely said "Hello" back.

"It's a nice day, today huh?" He asked. I replied, "Yes, it is."

Finally, the ride started moving, and I was ready. After several seconds into the ride, I felt the guy's hand on my knee. My heart began racing fast, and I became terribly uncomfortable, unsure of what to do. I shifted a little bit to the right to get closer to my brother, hoping the guy would take his hand off my knee. It did not work.

As the ride continued, it went inside an extremely dark tunnel. The darker we went into the tunnel, the closer the guy's hand got to my private area. By this time, I was so afraid that my body was frozen in fear. I prayed to God asking for the ride to end soon.

What should I do? Should I scream? Should I tell Jemonde? Should I tell him to get his hand off my private area? I was not sure what to do or say; I was young, only 14 years old.

My thoughts were interrupted as the ride began chugging up the hill. *Yes, the ride is almost over.* I said to myself. As the ride inched to the top of the hill in darkness, the guy's hand moved closer until his hand was in between my legs. Then the unexpected happened, he slid his hand under my shorts and inserted his finger inside of me. I felt so weak from fear that I began to feel faint.

I started praying harder, *Please, please, please get me off this ride*, I pleaded to God. After what seemed like an eternity, the ride came out of the dark tunnel and reached the top. I saw light peeking through, and the guy took his finger from inside of me. The ride quickly went down the hill. It was over, and my heart was beating so fast that I was having trouble breathing. The guy looked at me and said,

"That was fun huh?" and winked and gave me a sly grin. With my hands trembling, I unbuckled my seatbelt and as soon as the ride came to a complete stop, I jumped out.

As I left the ride, I wondered if I should tell my brother or even my family. I was embarrassed and ashamed, as if I had done something wrong. I grabbed Jemonde's hand and we walked back and met up with my parents. I never saw where the guy who did this to me went, but even 14 years later, I can remember how he looked and what he did to me. This creep scarred me for life and for the rest of my time at Universal Studios, I did not ride any more rides. I barely ate, and I watched my back at all times, fearful that something else might happen to me. In my typical fashion, I put on a façade and acted as if everything were okay.

I started blaming myself and I thought it was my fault this happened. Perhaps if I had not said hello to him, he would not have done that to me. Or, if I had been wearing pants instead of shorts, he would not have sexually assaulted me. Instead of blaming him, I was blaming me, and I felt miserable.

That night in the lobby of the hotel, Jemonde and I were relaxing on the couches. My mind was racing and I could not stop thinking about what transpired earlier that day. I was not really listening to what he was saying, and before I could take it back, I blurted out and said,

"A man sexually assaulted me on the Jurassic Park ride today."

Jemonde sat up straight and with a mad look on his face, said,

"WHAT?!" I looked down bashfully and continued,

"Yes, this happened on the Jurassic Park ride. Remember how you sat to the right of me and there was a white guy who sat to the left of me. I was in the middle of you two. Well..." my voice started to get softer.

"During the ride, he put his hand on my knee and as the ride continued, he inched his hand closer until he touched my private area. And he stuck his finger in me." I said, as the tears started to stream down my face.

My brother was heated. He loved me dearly and was very protective of me. He would risk his life to make sure I was okay. That's the kind of person he is. After a few minutes, he mustered up enough strength and said,

"You know what? I am so sorry you went through that, and I am glad you told me, especially now, emphasis on the word *now*. Because if you had told me this when we got off the ride, I would have tackled him to the ground and beat him up. No one messes with my sister, especially in that manner, and I might be in jail right now! Man, I can't believe that jerk did that. I cannot believe that happened to you." The whole time my brother kept shaking his head and saying, "He better be glad I didn't get to him."

Jemonde's presence and assurance made me feel better. He told me to not blame myself because by no means was it my fault. He went on to say that there are some sick people in this world. He even blamed himself by saying he should have sat next to the guy. It was not Jemonde's fault or my fault; it was only that creep's fault. I asked him not to say anything to Mom and Dad because I did not want them to know, just yet.

Even 11 years later when I went to Universal Studios and walked past that ride, the memory of what happened in 2002 came to my mind clearly, as if it had happened yesterday. I will never forget the day and that guy who changed my life for the worse.

Chapter 18

Struggling to Stay Alive

When I was 16 years old, I passed my driving exam and received my license. My parents told me that I was not to give anyone a ride in my car. They did it for safety and liability reasons. If I had a passenger in my car and got into an accident, a lawsuit could take place or injuries might occur, and my parents did not want to take that chance.

Now that I had a car, everyone wanted to be my friend, well those who were not embarrassed to ride in my car. I did not have the nicest car. It was an old, white Corsica and looked okay. Some students said,

"Aren't you embarrassed to drive that? I wouldn't be caught dead riding in something like that? Why can't yo parents get you something else." Several of the students who made these remarks did not even have a car, but they were bold enough to tell me how ugly mine was. I was driving and they were walking. Their mindset did not make much sense to me. However, the people who wanted a ride did not mind how my car looked.

One particular day, a student name *Destiny* who was older than me, yet two grades behind me in school, was persistent in her efforts to get me to take her somewhere.

"Please Tensie. I'll give you gas money." She pleaded.

"Sorry *Destiny*, I can't. I am not allowed to take anyone in my car." I said.

"Forget you then. You get yo' license and you think you betta than everyone else. I don't need a ride in your raggedy car anyway." She retorted.

She bugged me so much about giving her a ride, but my parents' words echoed in my mind. Finally, I gave in and gave *Destiny* a ride. After this, she told her friends I gave her a ride, and other students started asking me to take them places. I did not want to seem like a goody-two-shoes, as they called me, so a few times, I gave a couple students rides to get them off my back.

One afternoon, I had a terrible day at school. Students had bullied me badly that day, people were picking on my car, a girl who barely knew me called me an "ugly bitch," and a student had thrown vanilla ice cream in my hair during lunch. I was feeling extremely low and instead of going straight home, I decided to take a drive. I had no destination in mind; I just drove with tears in my eyes and my mind on so many things. After about 45 minutes, I ended up in Raleigh on New Hope Church Road and didn't even know it because I wasn't focused on the road.

As I drove, thoughts ran through my mind. Why are students so mean to me? Why am I only popular when people want something from me? Why are my eyes so big? Why do girls dislike me so much? Why this? Why that? At that moment, I contemplated ending my life. I wanted to kill myself, but I did not want people to know I killed myself. I wanted to make it seem like an accident, so I told myself, *Tensie, if you run this red light, you can end it all. The misery, pain, and suffering you feel now can soon be alleviated. You will no longer have to worry about people picking on you; you will no longer have to be afraid of going to school; you will not have to worry about someone sexually assaulting you ever again; you won't have to worry about students verbally and physically abusing you. You can escape all the heartache and pain you feel.*

I was so deep in my thoughts of ending it all and feeling sorry for myself that I almost ran the red light. I instantly snapped out of my trance and hit the brakes. My tires screeched loudly, and my car came to a jolting halt. After the light turned green, I pulled my car over to the side of the rode and started sobbing. I could not believe what I had tried to do. I almost killed myself because I was lost in my train of thought. How ironic that I wanted to kill myself and almost ended up killing myself because of the devil's thoughts in my mind. I cried like a baby for several minutes, and after I regained a clear mind, I turned around and drove back home. I realized I had so much to live for.

That night I thought heavily about the day's events and how I almost lost my life. Instead of thinking how much better off I would be if I were dead, I thought about how grateful I was to be alive. I thought about the many things that made me smile, the people who loved me and gave me hugs, how blessed I was to have two loving parents, and all the things that were going right in my life, and I began to slowly feel better. My good days outweighed my bad days, and although I thought about suicide, I could not go through with it. I did not want to leave my parents and family to mourn over me; I could not put them through that misery and pain. I kept praying and took things day by day.

I also did not want to give my bullies the satisfaction of knowing that because of their actions, I had taken my life. If I had done that, they would have gone on with their lives, and my parents would be left in sorrow and sadness. From then on, no matter how dark things got, I found hope and a ray of sunshine. The struggle to stay alive was tough, but in the end, I made it and I'm alive to share my story and give encouragement to others that there will be better days ahead if you keep the faith.

Chapter 19

Observations about My Race

Throughout my thirteen years of being bullied at school, I noticed that my own race, blacks, bullied me the most. In school, there was not one white or Latino student who bullied me; it was mainly my people who taunted and teased me. Black students called me sellout, Oreo, light bright damned near white, ugly, GEICO, big-eyed freak, high yellow, and other names. Students in my race threw my lunch on the cafeteria floor; the teacher who bullied me in fifth grade was a black woman; and the girls who picked up scissors and threatened to cut my hair in school were black. The stories I recounted in this book were done by black students. Many members from my race tore me down and belittled me, while the white students befriended and accepted me.

Colorism is a huge issue in the black race, and several girls who picked on me were of darker complexion. Colorism is defined as, "the tendency to perceive or behave toward members of a racial category based on the lightness or darkness of their skin tone" (Maddoxx & Gray, 2002). Based on this definition, this is how some darker-skinned girls behaved towards me. They shouted comments such as,

"You think you all that 'cuz you light skinned!"

Girls who did not even know me said,

"You act like a snob, just like a light-skinned bitch."

I even had a college professor, who was darker-skinned, tell me during class, "You don't realize how good you have it and how privileged you are because of how light your complexion is." These comments hurt deeply. I never rubbed the color of my skin in their faces or said I thought I was better because of my light complexion. They were internalizing the hate they had for themselves onto me.

Research suggests that "to some blacks, skin color discrimination is just as bitter as and more painful than racism. Some blacks perceive lighter skinned blacks as a snob, the self-anointed superior class of the race who considered themselves a cut above the darker-skinned blacks. This class and color consciousness is not uncommon in the South. Although racism has declined, colorism remains the same" (Hochschild, 2007). I can relate well to these researchers' findings, especially since I grew up in the South. I wish colorism were nonexistent. There are more important issues in this world than discussing the privileges or non-privileges based on the complexion of one's skin.

A second observation is that my race made fun of me for taking honors and advanced placement (AP) classes. I noticed that the higher I achieved in academia at my school, the less black students there were in my classes. In one of my AP classes, there was one other black student besides me. But for the most part, I was alone in these classes when it came to race. The good news is that because I was surrounded by white students in these classes, I was never bullied. However, I was embarrassed to be the only black person in my honors and AP classes because my race noticed this and made snide comments about how I was selling out to the white man.

"Why is you the only black in dat class?" my black peers asked me. "You in dere with all them white folks. You think you too good to be with us, huh?" They said.

Why did I have to be a sell out? Because I made good grades and was in AP and honors classes, I was not black enough? Why did my own race demean me so badly? When I think back to how these students talked, I laugh. They sounded so ignorant by saying, "you is." I shared these stories with Dad, and he said,

"You should tell them: you is dumb!" He laughed. The nerve of some of my black classmates to make fun of me for being in honors classes when they could barely speak proper English. Several black classmates thought it was cool to be dumb, and because I liked to learn, I was not cool and that is why they bullied me.

My race told me I was "acting white," a term used to reference blacks who use language or ways of speaking; display attitudes, behaviors, or preferences, or engage in activities considered to be white cultural norms (Bergin & Cooks, 2002; McArdle & Young, 1970; Neal-Barnett, 2001). The research shows that a distinct type of oppositionality to high achievement is racialized oppositionality in which peer taunts directed at black high achievers by other blacks include labels such as "oreo" or the charge of "acting white." In addition, socioeconomic status among whites and blacks determine achievement and those from lower socioeconomic statuses are more likely to ridicule the high achieving students (Bergin & Cooks, 2002; McArdle & Young, 1970; Neal-Barnett, 2001).

The research supports what I experienced in school. The black students who made fun of me and called me names such as "oreo" and sellout came from lower socioeconomic statuses. Many of the black students who picked on me lived in single parent homes and received free or reduced lunch. Yet, the black students who came from middle or upper class backgrounds and took honors and AP classes, were nice to me, and did not demean me or call me a sellout. The reason they did not do this is because we were on the same level, both academically and socioeconomically.

These are observations I made about my race while I was being bullied terribly at school. I love my people and am very proud to be a strong, black woman. We have a beautiful and unique culture, come in many shapes, sizes, and hues, come together on many important issues, and have a powerful history. However, just like with other races, there is work to be done in our race. One of the areas to improve in is to stop the "crabs in the barrel" mentality of bringing other blacks down because of the insecurity and inferiority some in my race feel. We need to become more united and stop saying that to perform well in school, on a job, or in life is to be a sellout and equated to being white. Intelligence is not based on race.

Chapter 20

I Have a Dream

"I say to you today my friends, so even though we face the difficulties of today and tomorrow. I still have a dream. It is a dream deeply rooted in the American dream..." -Rev. Dr. Martin Luther King, Jr.

These words echo in my head, and I can recite this speech at the drop of a dime. Mom and Dad taught my siblings and me this speech, in addition to other speeches, poems, and works of literature. My brother said these speeches at churches and traveled to various states to recite at conventions and banquets. I was mesmerized and wanted to learn speeches so I could travel and recite, too.

When I was four years old, Dad taught me Dr. King's, *I Have a Dream* speech. He was very patient with me and taught me the speech paragraph by paragraph. In one day, I learned it. With practice, rote, and elocution, within a week, I was solid in my delivery of the speech. I knew this speech from memory, which opened up a whole new world for me.

People from churches, convention centers, and banquets called my parents and asked me to recite at MLK events and Black History Month celebrations. I traveled in North Carolina and to Georgia, Virginia, and other states to perform. I was so short and small that every time I spoke, I stood on a chair with three to four phone books in the chair so people could see me over the podium. When I was introduced to the crowd, people chuckled. They wondered who this little person was who could recite. Some thought I was going to read the speech, but when they saw me stand in the chair on top of the phone books without a piece of paper in sight, they were spell bounded and wanted to see what I would do.

People were in awe that someone so young and small could recite such a powerful speech from memory! I might have been small, but I had a powerful voice. As soon as I began the speech, the room fell silent. People gawked at me in surprise that someone so young knew this speech from memory. People cried as I recited Dr. King's words because this speech resonated with them. They had experienced racism or had parents and grandparents who grew up during the days of segregation and Jim Crow. However, at four years old, I did not quite understand the meaning of the words, nor Dr. King's message. All I knew was that when I said the words *interposition* and *nullification*, people smiled, oohed and ahhed. How could this four year old know how to pronounce such big words?

In the beginning, I did not always pronounce these words properly, where I sometimes said "inposition and numfication." But people were so impressed that I knew the speech from memory that they always erupted in a round of applause. Mom taught me ebb and flow, the rise and fall of my voice to add emphasis to the speech. I added my own special touch by raising my hands at the end when I said, "Free at last, free at last, thank God almighty, we're free at last!" People immediately jumped to their feet and gave me a standing ovation. As I took my seat, people grabbed me to hug me, kiss me, and some pulled out their wallets and pocketbooks to give me a $1 or $5 bill. At four years old, I was making money and was doing so by the power of words.

When I first started speaking, I was shy and looked down at the floor the whole time, but Mom quickly fixed that.

"What are you looking at?" she asked.

"I'm scared to look at the people." I timidly replied.

"You have to engage your audience and keep people's attention. You do this by looking at them and having direct eye contact. Don't lose your audience by looking down." She said.

After that conversation and from then on, I held my head up as I spoke to the crowd. In the beginning, it was nerve-racking to look at the audience because I was so nervous. I began to question myself. Would people laugh at me? How many would smile at me? Would they giggle in my face? I knew that when I looked at the floor, I was safe because I did not see the facial expressions of the crowd. The floor would not laugh at me. I personified this object as my friend. But, Mom was right, and if I wanted to keep my audience's attention, I had to look at them and engage.

At the next events, I slowly raised my head and pretended to look at people's faces. I looked at their noses or the clock in the back of the room. As I progressed, practiced, and got better, I started looking at people directly in the eye. Mom's suggestion of holding up my head was perfect. When I looked at the audience, I was able to see their emotions. People smiled, laughed, cried, and I recognized how words, intonation, and inflection brought out many emotions in people.

One day in February 1995, I was asked to recite a speech during Black History Month. Renowned lawyer and North Carolina Central University alumnus Willie E. Gary was in attendance. I was not familiar with him or his accomplishments because I was only eight years old at the time, but Dad was excited that he was in the audience. He must have been someone powerful or popular, but I did not think much of it.

Because Dad was so excited, it made me even more excited, which helped with my delivery. The more excited I am before I speak, the better I do at speaking. This time, I brought down the house, and people gave me a thunderous applause. At the conclusion of the event, several people came up to me and shook my hand, wrote down my contact information to speak at future events, and gave me money as a congratulatory gift. Willie E. Gary was one of those people who came up to me. He shook my hand and said,

"Young lady, that was quite impressive! I am still in awe. I want to offer you a full scholarship to North Carolina Central University."

Dad stood there shocked, and I firmly shook his hand and said, "Thank you Mr. Gary! It is a pleasure to meet you sir."

Mr. Gary got my contact information from Dad and a few days later, I had a signed picture from Mr. Gary. In addition, actress Tonea Stewart from the show "In the Heat of the Night" came up and shook my hand, too. A few days later, I also received an autographed picture from her that said, "Don't Stop." At a young age, I learned the wonder of being kind to people and having personality. People were drawn to me, and it was because of how I treated them. People also liked hugging me because I was so small, but to be verbally offered a scholarship at eight years old from Mr. Gary is one of my proudest accomplishments.

Mr. Gary's and Ms. Stewart's words resonated with me then and continue to resonate with me today. Even though I was bullied badly at school because students said I could not dress and called me cruel names, in the eyes of my parents, family, lawyers, and celebrities, I was somebody. Celebrities knew me and were standing in line to shake my hand. However, these are experiences that students who bullied me cannot say. While they were finding new ways to torment me at school or bring me down, I was making my own money and starting a savings account. While they were making fun of me for not wearing name-brand shoes or clothes, I was adding money to my bank account. While my bullies were laughing at my parents' cars because they were not the nicest, my parents and I were staying in nice hotels and traveling. Those who picked on me hardly left the city, definitely not the state, and here I was, traveling throughout the United States. Instead of picking on me, they should have befriended me and could have traveled and experienced a fun life with me.

I understood the power of words. Words either uplifted individuals or tore down people; words inspired or demeaned. Words were the difference between life and death. The Bible says that there is power in the tongue, and I wanted my words to uplift, elevate, and bless others.

***

While I was a student at Terrell Lane Middle School, one of the teachers saw me perform the *I Have a Dream* speech. She liked my performance and asked Mom if I could recite the speech at an assembly program for the entire school during Black History Month. Mom said, "Sure, absolutely!"

Those were the worst two words I could have heard. I did not want to perform the speech at school because I knew students would make even more fun of me. I begged and pleaded for Mom to tell the teacher that she changed her mind and I would no longer be able to recite, but Mom was vehement.

"No, you are going to do this. I do not care what you think your classmates will think of you. This is an honor for you to perform in front of the whole school."

How ironic that I felt comfortable performing this speech in front of strangers, but I was terrified of performing the speech in front of people I knew (my classmates, teachers, and bullies). The dreadful day arrived, and I was miserable. As the Black History Month assembly began, there were several teachers who were a part of the program. My ears were on alert, and I could easily hear the comments from students.

"Oh my Godddddddddd. This is so boring!" *Shantel* said.

"Why am I here? I don't care nothing about Black History Month." *Jesse* replied.

These remarks came from black students. My own race did not care to hear or learn anything about their heritage and history. Hearing students' commentary made me feel worse, and I got butterflies in my stomach. I did not want to be seen as an outcast, so I tried blending in and acting nonchalantly right along with the students. We were seated on the floor in the cafetorium (half cafeteria, half auditorium), and I slouched down, put my head in my hand, looked bored, rolled my eyes, and acted as if I despised being there. In actuality, I was listening attentively to each word the speakers said to learn more about my heritage and history.

There were no printed programs so students did not know that I was on to recite. I wished, hoped, and prayed that time would run out so I would not have to speak. My thoughts were interrupted as I heard my name being called.

"Now, I present to you, Tensie Taylor, who will recite one of Dr. King's most famous speeches, *I Have a Dream*." my teacher said.

People began applauding, but all I heard was my classmates saying,

"What? Ugh! Not her again. Can she go somewhere and sit down? Why she always gotta be doin' something?"

Hearing these words negatively affected my concentration and confidence. I walked up on stage and did a poor job reciting the speech. I did not add any emphasis; I had no emotion in my face or voice. I recited the speech as if I did not want to be there, and people knew it. I was so boring that I bored my own self. I did not use my signature move of raising my hands at the end when I said, "Free at last, free at last." All I wanted to do was sit down, and my performance showed it.

"Thank God almighty, we are free at last." I turned around, handed the microphone to the teacher carelessly, and took my seat. At that moment, I wanted to cry. I wanted to cry because the look of disappointment on my mother's face made me feel terrible. I knew she was embarrassed by my performance and I was, too.

When I took my seat, nobody congratulated me, or said "good job." Not that I was expecting anyone to, but if one person had said it, my confidence might have been boosted. That made me feel even worse, but I knew I had done a poor job. I let the comments from my classmates get into my head, and it threw me off. Not to blame them for my performance, but instead of listening to their negative energy, I should have turned it into a positive by wowing them and shutting them up. Instead, I gave in and mimicked their behavior by not caring and acting like I did not want to be at the assembly. I let everyone down. Maybe if I had overheard one person say something nice, my performance would not have been so pitiful.

The earlier feeling I felt of wanting the assembly to end, I now felt the opposite. I no longer wanted the program to end because I knew I would have to face Mom. After we were dismissed, I went to the library, and just as I expected, Mom said,

"What kind of recitation was that?"

Bashfully and questioningly, I asked "What do you mean?"

"Don't play dumb with me. You not only embarrassed me, but you embarrassed yourself. You acted like you didn't want to perform and you didn't say the speech like you normally do."

I could only muster up a simple, "I'm sorry" because there was nothing else I could do or say. I had let Mom down, and I felt awful. That evening at home, Mom told Dad about my performance. He was shocked, too and could not believe it.

"Students threw off my concentration. They were saying mean things before I took the stage, and it affected my performance." I said trying to plead my case.

Dad said, "That is no excuse. You can't let what others say about you deter you from doing what is right or stop you from giving a stellar performance. Let this be a learning experience." Dad was a stern, yet fair person. He provided much sagacity, and was absolutely brilliant. He was small in stature, but big in discipline. I respected him so much, and his words continued to echo in my mind: *You can't let what others say about you deter you from giving a stellar performance.* Many years later, I would implement these words at a college function.

***

During my college days at North Carolina State University, I signed up and took advantage of any and every opportunity. The Eta Omicron chapter of Alpha Phi Alpha Fraternity, Inc. had an event called 1906 & Park, modeled after BET's 106 & Park. I applied to be a part of the show, and I was accepted.

To pay homage to Dr. King since he was an Alpha, I wanted to recite his speech and play and sing one of his favorite songs, "Precious Lord." During people's performances, I began to feel exactly how I felt when I was in the seventh grade. I wanted to do a mediocre job with my performance because I felt intimidated by the room full of students who were already making unnecessary comments about people's performances. During a student's performance, I snuck out and went outside to call Mom because I felt anxious.

"Mom, I cannot do this. Other people have been dancing, stepping, and playing the drums. No one is going to recite, and I know they will make fun of me. Nobody wants to hear me recite this speech. I should leave before they call my name." I said pleadingly.

In her comforting voice, she said,

"Listen, you can do this. Why? Because you bring a unique performance. You are reciting one of the most famous speeches and you are displaying three talents: reciting, singing, and playing the piano. As hard as this may be for you, do not worry about what other people are doing. Focus on what you are going to do and do it well."

I thanked her and hung up the phone. Her words comforted me, and my spirit and confidence were uplifted. I walked back inside as the program was still going. After the person who was on stage stopped performing, I heard my name.

"Ladies and gentleman, please welcome Tensie Taylor."

I walked up and took my seat on the couch. Before each person performed, we were interviewed by an Alpha and sat comfortably on the couch.

"Tensie, what are you going to do for us tonight?" *John* asked.

"I am going to recite Dr. King's *I Have a Dream* speech and sing and play one of his songs on my keyboard." I said.

Immediately I heard someone in the audience mumble,

"Well dang, how long is she going to be up there?"

Snickers and giggles followed this person's comment. I tried to ignore them as I remembered my mother and father's words. I proudly walked on stage and recited the *I Have a Dream* speech like I have never recited it before. One of the North Carolina State University staff members, Mama Thorpe, was beaming at me in the audience, which gave me the extra boost I needed. My elocution, delivery, and enunciation were on point, and when I concluded the speech, I was met with a round of applause. Next, I walked to the area where my keyboard and microphone were waiting for me, and began playing the song, Precious Lord. I sang from my soul and played powerfully and gave it my all, and after I was done, I received another round of applause. I had done it, and I felt great! Despite someone's comment earlier, I blocked out the negativity and did an awesome performance. If they had been there, my parents would have been proud of me!

Just as Dr. King had a dream, I too, have a dream. I dreamed of the day when people appreciated me for the content of my character and not made fun of me for the color of my skin or the size of my eyes. I dreamed that my race would encourage me, greet me with a smile, stand up for me when I was bullied, and not treat or talk to me in a demeaning or castigating tone. I dreamed of a life where I no longer felt afraid to go to school, where students didn't try to break my arm or push me into lockers or doors. I dreamed of a time where I would no longer pray to God and ask Him to make my eyes small because of the mean comments from students at school.

I dreamed that my book bag would no longer be yanked from my back or my articles thrown on the floor because I was too small and scared to stand up for myself. I dreamed of the day when I no longer had to pay a bully over $200 in hopes she would stop terrorizing me. I dreamed of the day when I would not be bullied out of a telephone booth in England or have that person bang on the booth and call me a derogatory name because I refused to get out when he told me to. I dreamed of the day when students no longer called me Oreo, GEICO, Glowworm, light bright, white, or banana. I dreamed of a day where students would no longer throw my awards on the floor after a ceremony or laugh at me because I preferred reading over watching television. I dreamed of the day where my classmates would become more united and would not pick on me because I did not wear name-brand shoes or clothes or envy me because I lived in a nice home.

I dreamed of the day where I no longer was afraid to go to school because of what someone would say or do to me. I dreamed of the day when my peers would say, "I'm proud of you! Good job Tensie!" I dreamed of the day where I would no longer have a bag of potato chips thrown at me on the bus or ice cream thrown in my hair in the cafeteria at school. I dreamed of the day where I was no longer made fun of for being short, small, or flat-chested. I dreamed of the day when I would no longer cry myself to sleep at night. I dreamed of a day where I would walk into a room and people would say, "Thank you Tensie for helping me" instead of bringing me down. I dreamed of the day where I no longer felt depressed or contemplated suicide. I dreamed of the day where I would make a difference in people's lives, and the people who once bullied me would now respect me.

In 2016, some of my dreams have come to fruition. Those individuals who cut me deeply with their words, hands, and actions are now trying to befriend me. Students who bullied me in school have sent me Facebook messages apologizing for their behavior. That little girl who once was so self-conscious about my eyes and body is now proud to be who I am. The old me who was once depressed and thought about killing herself is now happy with life and makes sure to spread love and encouragement to others.

I have forgiven those students who bullied and tormented me, not for them, but for me. I have no animosity or ill will towards them, and although I forgave them, I have not forgotten what they did. These individuals may have tried to break my arm and heart, but they did not break my spirit.

Life is interesting. People who bullied me in school and told me I would not amount to anything are the ones I see hanging on the streets when I come home to North Carolina to visit. The guys who made fun of me by calling me ugly and saying I did not have a shape are now the same guys messaging me through social media asking for a date. The people who made fun of me because I wore skips and did not have name-brand clothes are the ones who barely graduated high school and are living at home with their parents. The people who belittled me and told me I would not amount to anything in life are now serving me at McDonald's. The students who mercilessly picked on me in school for being skinny and calling me anorexic are now twice the size they were in high school and are suffering from obesity, while I am still petite.

Perhaps if the students who bullied me had focused more on their schoolwork and spent less time picking on me or even befriended me, they might have graduated from high school and done something productive with their lives. The people who made fun of me because I chose to study in school instead of party are now struggling to make ends meet. My intention is not to bring these people down for the choices they made or the lifestyle they live now, but I find it ironic that those who bullied and wished failure on me in school are now the ones who are not as successful as they could be. They told me I would not amount to much in life, and yet, they ended up setting themselves up for failure.

I tell people to never laugh at someone's dream or make fun of another individual because (s)he is different because one never knows what that person is going through or who (s)he will become in life. People laughed at me and the dreams I told them, and guess where that got them? Nowhere. I am living my dream and everything I wanted to come to fruition has because I have been prayerful, worked hard, and sacrificed to make it all possible. I could easily laugh at my bullies because of where they are now, but I do not because I am a bigger person than that. Be careful how you treat people because the ones you step over now might be the ones you need later in life.

As funny as it sounds, I thank my bullies. I thank them for one reason only: for showing me how to *never* treat anyone. My bullies ridiculed, belittled, criticized, abused, and demeaned me. Because of their iniquitous behavior, I made sure to never treat any human being that way, and I have held true to this promise.

Chapter 21

Thank You

Vince Lombardi once said, "The only place success comes before work is in the dictionary." To become successful in life, people must work hard, make sacrifices, and block out the negativity from naysayers and doubters. These are all parts of the ingredients for success. The words of my doubters served as more motivation for me to excel. I am perplexed by my bullies' way of thinking. I was a straight-A student, involved in extracurricular activities, participated in volunteerism, and was a well-rounded student, and yet, they said I would not amount to anything in life. Their logic was way off.

What I later learned in life is that the hate and jealousy my bullies had for me was internal. By their saying I would not amount to anything in life, they were speaking of themselves. We had the same teacher, the same number of hours in the day, the same text books, and yet, I was doing remarkably well and they were the ones failing classes, getting kicked out of school, and being suspended. They were on a bad path and tried to bring me down with them. I refused to follow the crowd and instead took the road less traveled.

I have succeeded against the odds because of my perseverance, determination, and strong, unequivocal desire to prove everyone who ever wished failure on me wrong. I would not have succeeded without those individuals in my corner who told me to keep the faith and to keep on pushing.

To my loving parents, thank you for instilling in me that with faith, prayer, hard work, determination, and education, I can become anything I want in life. You both are an inspiration to me, and because of your humble beginnings, you made a way for yourselves and for us. I will forever be grateful to both of you for your tough love and unending support.

Mom and Dad, I also thank you for exposing me to opportunities, for sacrificing what you had in order to make my life easier. Thank you for showing me the importance of education and how it can never be taken away from me. Thank you for the family vacations, the fun times in the pool, the historic places we visited, and the awesome places we traveled. Thank you for treating me like a princess and never giving up on me. Thank you for drying my tears and giving me hugs. Thank you for saving my life. I am sure as you read this book, you learned things you did not know about me or what I went through, but it was your love and dedication that kept me going. I could have easily given up on life, but when I thought about the trials and tribulations you went through and how you had it much harder than me and still persevered, I knew I could do to it, too. I have the Taylor and Richardson blood running through my veins, and we are not quitters or losers. We are winners and are people who work hard. Thank you for all you have done for me.

I am thankful for the few spankings I received because it kept me in line. Because of Mom's infamous flip flop, I am where I am today. I also thank Mom and Dad for teaching me respect and manners, how to say yes ma'am, no ma'am, yes sir, no sir, please and thank you. I thank them for showing me how to treat everyone the same, regardless if the individual is the janitor, custodial worker, street sweeper, dean of a college, or president of the United States, each person deserves to be treated with dignity and respect.

To my brother Jemonde, thank you for being the best brother in the world. Thank you for helping me with my homework, visiting me during summer camps, making me laugh, protecting me, and being a provider like my father. Thank you for showing me how a man should treat a lady; thank you for helping me with Calculus in college; thank you for being patient with me, and thank you for showing me how to treat people. Through your life and ministry, I have learned so much about you, from how you interact with an infant to how you share the same colloquialism as an eighty-year old man. You have the gift to converse with anyone, whether large or small, young or old, intelligent or barely educated, you interact with all people the same. I thank you for sharing your pictures and stories about your journey to Europe and Africa. You showed me the importance of international travel, and because of this, I was able to travel to these continents. I also thank you for giving me resources and suggestions on how to raise funds for these trips. You are the true definition of a role model.

Jemonde, I thank you for letting me be your shadow by following you everywhere you went, asking you fifteen million questions, and teaching me how to play basketball and golf. Even though I never became the shortest point guard in history, I still learned how to play golf, and I am a pro on the miniature golf course. Although I am right handed, you helped me become ambidextrous by teaching me how to play golf with my left hand. Thank you for showing me how to play the piano and trumpet, but most importantly, thank you for not laughing when I first started playing. I know I sounded like an animal dying, but you were patient with me, and taught me new tricks that I did not learn in band class. In essence, thank you for being you.

To my sister Kelise, thank you for teaching me how to dress. You took me shopping when I entered high school and helped me with my style, and I appreciate you for this. Thank you for showing me how to put on eyeliner. This helped in my quest to make my eyes appear smaller and for me to feel more beautiful. Thank you for showing me how to use makeup. But most importantly, thank you for standing up for me when students made comments about me during the award's day ceremonies. It means so much to know that you had my back, and I enjoyed seeing your smiling face in the audience during award's day.

To my wonderful teachers and professors along the way, thank you for giving me the gift of education. You do not get enough credit for the work you do in enriching students' lives and helping them become the professions they choose in life, but I salute all of you. If it had not been for you, I would not be where I am today.

I thank each person who was my true friend and who majorly influenced and played a role in my life. I thank you for your hugs, kisses, donations, words of encouragement, tough love, and unending support. Thank you for cheering me on the sidelines; thank you for picking me up when I fell; and thank you for playing such a pivotal role in my life. I can never repay all the individuals who influenced me, but I will pay it forward by lending a helping hand to as many people as I can.

Because of the good and the bad, the ups and downs, the twists and turns through this journey called life, I am the woman I am today. Each experience whether positive or negative has molded and shaped me into the individual I am. One thing I learned is that having bad days makes you appreciate the good ones even more. If there were no rain, we would never appreciate the sun. Life only gets more challenging along the way, but when I think back to where I have come, and where I am going, the only thing I can do is smile.

Chapter 22

Fighting Back

To those who are being bullied or have been bullied, I empathize with you. Many times people ask me, "How did you survive?" My answer is, "It was hard, but I made it." I thought about how much it would hurt my family if I committed suicide, and how those who bullied me would go on to live their happy lives, and I was not going to let that happen. Each day was a challenge, some more challenging than others, but I look at where I am today, and every hurdle I faced, every obstacle I jumped over made me Tensie J. Taylor. It made me a stronger person and it taught me how to fight back, not with fists or weapons, but with words and education. Now, I'm a little firecracker. Tell me I can't do something, and I will show you I can.

I survived because I told adults what was going on at school. Whether it was my parents, teachers, or administrators at school, I told someone. Even though I may not have told adults everything I experienced, some knew what I was going through. If you are being bullied, tell an adult immediately.

One thing I would do differently is I would ask my parents to enroll me in martial arts classes. That way, I could have fought back when a student physically harmed me. If I had known Tae Kwon Do or had a black belt, that student who tried to break my arm might have gotten her arm broken. I am not condoning violence, but in situations where a student is being physically terrorized, martial arts would come in handy. Parents, consider enrolling your children in martial arts classes if they are bullied at school.

Even though I did not stand up for myself at school for fear of what a bully would do to me, now, I have the gumption to stand up, and I stand up with words. I remember an instance in college when I wore a Tommy Hilfiger shirt. A student came up to me and said,

"Tensie, I hope you know you're wearing a designer who said he doesn't want black people wearing his clothes." She paused and continued, "Oh, but wait, YOU ain't Black!" She then burst into laughter.

The old, timid me from secondary school would have stood there and not said anything. But the new me, the person who was now fighting back with words retorted,

"I see you think you're funny, huh? Well, what's funny to me is that I can afford to wear his clothes and you can't, probably because I have more money in my account since I'm here on a full academic scholarship, and you're not."

She immediately stopped laughing, and the people around her who were once laughing at me, were now laughing at her. She got up, rolled her eyes, and walked off. I was still amazed how people could say mean things and joke about me, but as soon as I made a comment (a truthful one) about them, they looked like they wanted to cry. This student never made a comment about me or my clothes again. People could dish it but certainly couldn't take it.

A few years later after I graduated with my master's degree in education from the USC Rossier School of Education, I received a phone call about having an in person interview for a job at USC. I wanted to present myself in the best possible light, so I wore a nice, black business suit, researched the department, brought my personality and charm, and was ready for the interview.

The lady who interviewed me was a Latina, and she asked,

"Where do you see yourself in 10 years?"

I replied, "I see myself having received my doctorate in education and serving as Vice Chancellor for Student Affairs at a university in California."

After my response, she began laughing. With a look of disdain on my face, I asked,

"Is something funny?"

With a smirk on her face, she said, "You really think you can do that?"

By this time, I was heated, but I tried to contain my composure, and I fought back with words.

"No I do not *think* I can accomplish this, I *know* I can. My master's degree from this prestigious university coupled with my five years' work experience in diversity, admissions, and college access at three universities, along with my experience working for the President of the universities in North Carolina and the Vice Provost for Diversity and Equity at North

Carolina State University, in addition to my extracurricular activities and more than 300 awards I have won in life, make me qualified and determined to do the job of Vice Chancellor in ten years. And furthermore, when people, such as yourself, laugh at my dreams, you're only doing me a favor by giving me more motivation to prove people like you wrong. Thank you for your time. Please have a great afternoon."

The interviewer looked stunned, and I stood up with my head held high and walked out. The next day, I received a phone call, and they offered me the job. Needless to say, I turned it down. The audacity of the interviewer to laugh at my dream was shocking. What was even funnier was that I could have laughed at her. I was dressed appropriately with professional attire, and she had on sweatpants and a sweatshirt. However, I stood up for myself, fought back with words, and left the interviewer speechless. I did not use any profanity or raise my voice. In a calm tone, I put that woman in her place and fought back with my words, education, and experience.

After I graduated from North Carolina State University with my bachelor's in communication and minor in psychology, I was granted a job interview at a company in Cary. The lady who interviewed me was white, and I felt she was prejudiced against me because I was black. As the interview began, she asked me if I had experience answering phones and sending emails, and I said I did. Out of nowhere, she rudely says,

"Do you want this job or not?"

I was taken aback because not only was I answering her questions, but I was providing concrete examples of the work I had done. She then looked at my resume and saw that I was the first place winner in an oratorical contest. She said, "What's oratorical?"

In my head, I'm thinking, *this lady does not know what oratorical means, yet has the audacity to look down on me during this interview.* At that moment, I used every huge vocabulary word I could think of such as vivacity, verisimilitude, gargantuan, assiduous. I knew that if she did not know what oratorical meant, she would not know what any of the words I used meant. After I laid out her soul with my vocabulary words, the lady looked at me in shock; I guess it was hard for her to fathom that a little black girl knew such big words when she probably didn't know any of the meanings herself. She had nothing to say and moved on to the next question.

"Did you really go to England? Do you really know how to type 140 words per minute? Did you really travel to Africa? Did you really work in the Chancellor's office when you were a student?" Her interview was insulting. She did not ask me to expound upon my experiences or to tell her about a time when I led a project. Instead, she questioned everything on my resume, as if I had lied and made it all up. She was insulting me and my intelligence, and I was mad.

Instead of telling her about herself and using profanity, I fought back with my words, academic abilities, study abroad opportunities, and extracurricular involvement. I left this woman speechless.

After having these experiences, I recollected the stories my parents shared about the obstacles they faced. Dad grew up during segregation in the south and had to walk 5 miles a day to school: 2.5 miles to school and 2.5 miles from school. He was not allowed to ride the school bus because only white kids rode the bus. He mentioned that sometimes the bus driver saw him walking on the road and to be mean, he deliberately ran into a big, puddle after it rained to splash him. Nonetheless, Dad kept walking to school because he knew that education was his way out of poverty. Even when it rained, snowed, or was extremely hot, Dad walked to school because he had a hunger and thirst for knowledge. Dad was called every rude name except for sir or Mr. After he graduated from high school, he was not allowed to go to certain colleges because of the color of his skin.

Mom, too, faced discrimination and hardship while growing up. She had to enter through the back of the store, and she had to wear her siblings' hand-me-downs because her parents were dirt poor. When Mom started high school, she had a D- grade point average because she had to help on the farm and could only go to school when it rained. She worked on the farm to bring in money for her parents and siblings.

When she came home from school, she could not immediately start on her homework until she fed the chickens, milked the cows, and fixed dinner. When she studied her lessons, she did so by candlelight because they did not have electricity. Mom could have used every excuse to not succeed, but she used this as more motivation to achieve, and graduated at the top of her high school class. Mom was determined and she did not have anyone to help her. Her mother, my grandmother, had a third grade education, so she was unable to help Mom. Yet, what my grandparents lacked in education, they made up for in wisdom. They were very sagacious and astute because they had traveled the road called life. My parents graduated from high school and college and worked assiduously to get themselves out of poverty. They went on to become phenomenal individuals.

I learned a plethora of information from my parents, but what I learned most is the power of education and perseverance. When I finally found my voice, I began fighting back with words, and once I started, no one could stop me. I encourage those who are bullied to find your voice. You can find your voice by confiding in an adult about the bullying you are enduring. If you need to seek out counselors to help you cope with the trauma you face, by all means, please do. Therapy helps the healing process and teaches you how to cope with situations and tragedies. I ask that students who witness another student being bullied to be an ally by standing up. Do not join in the banter and laugh. Stand up for this student because you might just save a life.

If people would be kinder, gentler, and nicer to each other, our world would be a better place. If you do not like or agree with someone, you do not have to comment or bring them down to elevate yourself. Individuals are bullied because of sexual orientation, socioeconomic status, race, color, religion, creed, national origin, sex, age, physical or mental disability, veteran status, citizenship, genetic information, and more. Instead of physically or verbally harming another person because (s)he is different from you, I challenge you to embrace the differences and learn from this person because it might enlighten you on things you never knew or understood.

Chapter 23

My Accomplishments

I have been through so many challenges in my life, but I am still standing. I thank God for giving me the strength, determination, resiliency, tenacity, and perseverance to keep going. Despite what I have been through, I continue to have a smile on my face and encourage anyone I can.

I am very proud of my accomplishments. To live in fear almost daily because of the bullying I faced at school and to come out on top brings me great pride and joy. Please allow me to share my accomplishments with you, not to brag, but to show you that when you are determined, no one or anything can stand in your way.

I graduated from Louisburg High School with a 4.4 grade point average, and during my school years, I was active in clubs and extracurricular activities, such as the Yearbook Committee, Quiz Bowl team, Battle of the Books, a mentor, a peer mediator, a tutor, trumpet player in the band, class president, long distance and hurdle runner in track and field, cheerleader, member of Future Business Leaders of America, and participated in school plays. I sang in the choir at my church, Hickory Grove Baptist Church, and led solos. I participated in volunteer opportunities in Franklin County, such as picking up trash along the highway, visiting nursing homes in Louisburg, singing to the elderly, volunteering at the Ronald McDonald house and playing the piano, and speaking to young people at schools and churches. I have more than 150 trophies, plaques, and medallions in addition to more than 180 certificates and pins. My awards are in the areas of academics, sports, essay contests, singing contests, piano recitals, speaking engagements, study abroad opportunities, and more. I have received awards from mayors in North Carolina and California, and have been honored alongside celebrities.

At 16 years old, I traveled abroad to England, Ireland, Wales, and Scotland for the People to People Student Ambassador Program. This program was founded by President Dwight D. Eisenhower to expose young people to the cultures, customs, and beliefs of other countries in hopes of bringing more people together. I was the only person selected from my county to go on this trip. While in these countries, I visited Stratford-upon-Avon (Shakespeare's birthplace), kissed the Blarney Stone in Ireland (which brings good luck), rode the London Eye, visited Buckingham Palace, and saw the Tower of London. I had the opportunity to play the grand piano in Westminster Cathedral Hall for Queen Elizabeth's Knight, Sir Andrew. I played different genres including classical, rhythm and blues, and gospel all from memory. I play the piano by music and by ear.

At 19, I traveled to Ghana, West Africa during the country's 50th independence. I met African kings of the village, walked through the door of no return, visited the slave castles, learned my Ghanaian name (Akua because I was born on a Wednesday), learned an African dance, met the US Ambassador to Ghana, went to a school called Kokobrite, and visited the birthplace of W.E.B. DuBois. This trip cost more than $5,000, and I raised all the funds through monetary donations.

At 25, I traveled to Beijing, China to study the similarities and differences of the education system of China and the United States. I climbed the Great Wall, saw a Kung Fu show, participated in an acrobat show, ate local food, went on a tuktuk ride, visited Beijing Normal University, Peking University, and Capital Normal University, participated in a lavish Chinese dinner, and more.

At 26, I traveled to Guatemala on an Alternative Spring Break trip with students from the University of Southern California to help a school in an impoverished area. We built a principal's office, repaired the roof on the school, and taught English to the Guatemalan students. We donated clothes, toys, stuffed animals, books, markers, pens, and more. I love giving back and helping others by donating my time, talent, and treasure.

At 27, I traveled to Dubai and visited the Grand Mosque in Abu Dhabi, went to Ferrari World Theme Park, wore a hijab, rode a camel, and visited the Burj Khalifa (the tallest building in the world). In all, at 28 years old, I have traveled to 17 countries, five continents, and will visit Australia by the end of 2016.

Even though people tried to tear me down with their words, harmed me with their physical abuse, called me ugly and cruel names, and said I would not amount to anything in life, I persevered and survived. Not only do I play the piano and trumpet, I sing both soprano and alto, and play an instrument called the omnichord. I have played the piano for over 20 years and have played the trumpet for 16 years. I have played and sung at weddings, celebrations, and conventions and even played the piano in Accra, Ghana.

In 2009 at the age of 21, I graduated from North Carolina State University from the College of Humanities and Social Sciences with a degree in Communication and a minor in Psychology. During my college years, I held four internships at: (1) Nortel Networks in Employee Communications; (2) IBM in Technical Writing; (3) Blue Cross Blue Shield of North Carolina in Diversity Consulting, and (4) Progress Energy in Marketing Consulting.

My first job after college was working with the President of the University of North Carolina's General Administration System, Erskine Bowles, where I worked on committees to help increase community college access for students and researched ways to reduce the achievement gap. I then worked at my alma mater, North Carolina State University for the Vice Provost for Equity and Diversity as a Diversity Program Coordinator, where I planned programs to increase awareness on diversity and cultural issues to students, faculty, staff, administrators, and community members.

In 2012 at the age of 25, I moved to Los Angeles, California to pursue a master's degree and in May 2014, I graduated with a Master of Education in Postsecondary Administration and Student Affairs from the University of Southern California's Rossier School of Education. I now work at the University of Southern California as the Assistant Director of the Black Alumni Association.

In addition to my career in education, I am also involved in the entertainment industry. I am a red carpet host for the online network, Rich Girl Network.TV, and have had the pleasure of meeting and interviewing more than 300 celebrities at more than 150 red carpet events in Hollywood since my three years of living in Los Angeles. I have attended the People's Choice Awards, Grammys, Oscars, NAACP Image Awards, BET Awards, and numerous other Hollywood award shows. At the Grammy's, I sat behind Beyoncé' and Jay-Z and was surrounded by the hottest musicians, such as John Legend, Taylor Swift, Pink, Daft Punk, Pharrell, and more. I have met Oprah, Angela Bassett, Russell Simmons, Sanaa Lathan, LL Cool J, Vanna White, Alex Trebek, Dick Van Dyke, John Amos, Boris Kodjoe, Nicole Ari Parker, Nigel Lythgoe, Pat Sajack, Cody Walker, Caleb Walker, Nick Cannon, Tatiyana Ali, Tamera Mowry, Tina Lawson, Tyrese, Kevin Hart, Michael Ealy, and countless other celebrities. I even had the pleasure of sharing my bullying story with the beautiful actress, model, and singer Christina Milian.

I have been a contestant on Wheel of Fortune, appeared in the movie *Whitney*, been on the show CW's *Hatched*, filmed for a feature film entitled CainAbel, appeared in four shorts, and interviewed for a web series at a beautiful mansion in Bel-Air. In addition, I have been interviewed on radio shows, in magazines, and newspapers. My story *From oppressed to success* was published in Chicken Soup for the Soul: Think Possible's book in October 2015, and now I have written my first book. I have accomplished so much in 28 years of life, and I know I will accomplish even more!

Chris Brown once said in a song, "Look at me now." I echo this statement, not in a cocky way, but in a confident manner. Those who bullied me in school are now the ones running up to me when they see me when I am home in North Carolina. Those who said I would not amount to anything in life are now asking me to get an autograph of their favorite celebrity. Those people who said I was ugly are now telling me how beautiful I look standing next to Angela Bassett. Those who picked on me for having big eyes are now looking at me on the big screen. The list goes on. If I had given up years ago, I would not be where I am today. If I had tried to fit in with the crowd, I would be where those people are: nowhere. Because of God's grace and mercy, I am still here. I am happy. I am alive, and I am sharing my story with the world.

Chapter 24

From Terror to Triumph

Bullying is an epidemic, and people are bullied all over the world. Many young people are committing suicide because of being bullied at school and on social media. I can imagine what these people go through. I thank God that social media or the internet was not as popular when I was a child. I did not have to deal with Facebook, Twitter, or Instagram posts from bullies because that was not the generation I grew up in. However, I did deal with constant verbal abuse, physical abuse, and fear of what would happen at school.

All of my days at school were not bad. I had good days, great times, and several fond memories. My good days outweighed my bad, but the dark days I had will forever be etched in my mind. Yet, I kept the faith, persevered, and did not give up, and because of this, I am where I am today.

The vulnerability of my story is to bring hope and inspiration to those who read this book, especially those who are bullied at home, school, church, or anywhere else. Even as an adult, I continue to face instances of bullying. I had a supervisor once throw a menu in my face because she did not like the selection I made. I had another supervisor curse me out for making a mistake. I had a neighbor constantly leave provocative notes on my car and when I told him to stop, he slashed my tire.

I once had a guy leave a note on my car calling me an ignorant punk. I had a male in my neighborhood stand in a parking space on the street to prevent me from parking in front of his house, even though I lived on a public street. I had a car tailgate me on the highway and then pass and sideswipe my car because I let myself in front of her car on the freeway. I had a coworker verbally bully me because I refused to do her work. I even had a random person curse me out on Twitter and call me ugly because of a picture I posted.

As you can see, in adulthood, bullying continues, and I am sure you, the reader, can add a story about a time you were bullied. As badly as I want this epidemic to end, I am not sure if it will. The only way bullying will end is when people keep their mouths closed if they don't have anything nice to say and their hands to themselves if they don't like someone. There needs to be more anti-bullying programs and initiatives. Positively speaking, once people learn to love more and be accepting of those who are different from them, then and only then will the bullying stop.

Until that day comes, to those who are bullied, stand up for yourself and try your best to fight back in a non-violent way. It may be hard to turn the other cheek, but it is possible to do. I did.

From terror to triumph, I survived being bullied, and with God, determination, perseverance, mentors, resources, and the right people in your corner, you can make it, too. As my Dad always says, "Keep the faith!"

Statistics on Bullying

- Nearly 1 in 3 students (27.8%) report being bullied during the school year (National Center for Educational Statistics, 2013).

- 19.6% of high school students in the US report being bullied at school in the past year. 14.8% reported being bullied online (Center for Disease Control, 2014).

- 64% of children who were bullied did not report it; only 36% reported the bullying (Petrosina, Guckenburg, DeVoe, and Hanson, 2010).

- More than half of bullying situations (57%) stop when a peer intervenes on behalf of the student being bullied (Hawkins, Pepler, and Craig, 2001).

- School-based bullying prevention programs decrease bullying by up to 25% (McCallion and Feder, 2013).

- The reasons for being bullied reported most often by students were looks (55%), body shape (37%), and race (16%) (Davis and Nixon, 2010).

- The effects of bullying are tragic. Students who experience bullying are at increased risk for depression, anxiety, sleep difficulties, and poor school adjustment (Center for Disease Control, 2012).

- Students who bully others are at increased risk for substance use, academic problems, and violence later in adolescence and adulthood (Center for Disease Control, 2012).

- Compared to students who only bully, or who are only victims, students who do both suffer the most serious consequences and are at greater risk for both mental health and behavior problems (Center for Disease Control, 2012).

- Students who experience bullying are twice as likely as non-bullied peers to experience negative health effects such as headaches and stomachaches (Gini and Pozzoli, 2013)

- 50% of young people have bullied another person, 30% of which do it at least once a week.

- 69% of young people have witnessed somebody else being bullied, 43% of which see it at least once a week.

- 43% of young people have been bullied, 44% of which are bullied at least once a week.

- Appearance is cited as the number 1 aggressor of bullying, with 51% saying they were bullied because of attitudes towards how they look.

- 26% said their weight was targeted, 21% body shape, 18% clothing, 14% facial features, 9% glasses and 8% hair color.

- 23% females with ginger hair cited their hair color as the bullying aggressor.

- Overall, 47% of young people want to change their appearance. 48% want teeth whitening, 17% breast implants, 6% liposuction and 5% botox.

- 74% of those who have been bullied, have, at some point been physically attacked. 17% have been sexually assaulted. 62% have been cyber bullied.

- As a result of bullying, 29% self-harm, 27% skipped class, 14% developed an eating disorder and 12% ran away from home.

- Highest risks to bullying were the following groups: all types of disability, LGBT, and low income backgrounds.

- 40% of respondents reported being bullied for personal appearance 36% reported being bullied for body shape, size and weight.

- Of those who were bullied, 98% were bullied by another student, 17% from a sibling, 13% from a teacher and 8% from their parents/guardians.

- 55% report bullying. 92% to a teacher, 49% were satisfied. 86% to a family member, 82%

were satisfied. 69% to a friend, 72% were satisfied.

- 45% did not report bullying. 32% of which felt it would not be taken seriously, 32% were too embarrassed and 26% were scared of it getting worse.

- Those who have bullied were more likely to be in trouble with the police (36%) vs. witnesses to bullying (23%) and those who have been bullied (22%).

- 45% of young people experience bullying before the age of 18.

- 36% of young people aged 8 to 22 are worried about being bullied at school, college or university.

- 38% believe their school, university or college doesn't take bullying seriously.

- More than 16,000 young people are absent from school because of bullying.

- 83% of young people say bullying has a negative impact on their self-esteem.

- 30% of young people have gone on to self-harm as a result of bullying.

- 10% of young people have attempted to commit suicide as a result of bullying.

- Those who have been bullied are more than twice as likely to have difficulty in keeping a job, or committing to saving compared to those not involved in bullying.

- People who have been bullied are at greatest risk for health problems in adulthood, over six times more likely to be diagnosed with a serious illness, smoke regularly, or develop a psychiatric disorder compared to those not involved in bullying.

- Over the last three years, there has been an 87% increase in the number of Childline's counseling sessions about online bullying.

- 40% of 7 to 11 year old respondents know someone who has been cyberbullied.

- 7 in 10 young people aged between 13 and 22 have been a victim of cyberbullying.

- An estimated 5.43 million young people in the UK have experienced cyberbullying, with 1.26 million subjected to extreme cyberbullying on a daily basis.

- Over two in five gay pupils who experience homophobic bullying attempt or think about taking their own life as a direct consequence.

- Three in five young people say that bullying has a direct impact on their school work and straight-A students have told us it makes them want to leave education entirely.

- More than half (55%) of lesbian, gay and bisexual young people experience homophobic bullying in Britain's schools.

- Almost 99% hear phrases such as 'that's so gay' or 'you're so gay' in school.

- More than one third of adolescents report bullying bias-based school bullying (Russell, Sinclair, Poteat, and Koenig, 2012).

- Bias-based bullying is more strongly associated with compromised health than general bullying (Russell, Sinclair, Poteat, and Koenig, 2012).

- Race-related bullying is significantly associated with negative emotional and physical health effects (Rosenthal et al, 2013)

- 81.9% of students who identify as LGBTQ were bullied in the last year based on their sexual orientation (National School Climate Survey, 2011).

- Peer victimization of all youth was less likely to occur in schools with bullying policies that are inclusive of LGBTQ students (Hatzenbuehler and Keyes, 2012).

- 63.5% of students feel unsafe because of their sexual orientation, and 43.9% because of their gender expression (National School Climate Survey, 2011).

- 31.8% of LGBTQ students missed at least one entire day of school in the past month because they felt unsafe or uncomfortable (National School Climate Survey, 2011).

- 64% of students enrolled in weight-loss programs reported experiencing weight-based victimization (Puhl, Peterson, and Luedicke, 2012).

- One third of girls and one fourth of boys report weight-based teasing from peers, but prevalence rates increase to approximately 60% among the heaviest students (Puhl, Luedicke, and Heuer, 2011).

- 84% of students observed students perceived as overweight being called names or getting teased during physical activities (Puhl, Luedicke, and Heuer, 2011).

- There is a strong association between bullying and suicide-related behaviors, but this relationship is often mediated by other factors, including depression and delinquency (Hertz, Donato, and Wright, 2013).

- Youth victimized by their peers were 2.4 times more likely to report suicidal ideation and 3.3 times more likely to report a suicide attempt than youth who reported not being bullied (Espelage and Holt, 2013).

- Students who are both bullied and engage in bullying behavior are the highest risk group for adverse outcomes (Espelage and Holt, 2013).

- Bullied youth were most likely to report that actions that accessed support from others made a positive difference (Davis and Nixon, 2010).

- Actions aimed at changing the behavior of the bullying youth (fighting, getting back at them, telling them to stop, etc.) were rated as more likely to make things worse (Davis and Nixon, 2010).

- Students reported that the most helpful things teachers can do are: listen to the student, check in with them afterwards to see if the bullying stopped, and give the student advice (Davis and Nixon, 2010).

- Students reported that the most harmful things teachers can do are: tell the student to solve the problem themselves, tell the student that the bullying wouldn't happen if they acted differently, ignore what is going on, or tell the student to stop tattling (Davis and Nixon, 2010).

- As reported by students who have been bullied, the self-actions that had some of the most negative impacts (telling the person to stop/how I feel, walking away, pretending it doesn't bother me) are often used by youth and often recommended to youth (Davis and Nixon, 2010).

- Bystanders' beliefs in their social self-efficacy were positively associated with defending behavior and negatively associated with passive behavior from bystanders – i.e. if students believe they can make a difference, they're more likely to act (Thornberg et al, 2012)

- Students who experience bullying report that allying and supportive actions from their peers (such as spending time with the student, talking to him/her, helping him/her get away, or giving advice) were the most helpful actions from bystanders (Davis and Nixon, 2010).

- Students who experience bullying are more likely to find peer actions helpful than educator or self-actions (Davis and Nixon, 2010).

- If you are thinking of committing suicide, please call the National Suicide Prevention Lifeline immediately at 1-800-273-8255. They are available 24 hours a day, 7 days a week.

References

Suicide Prevention
National Suicide Prevention Lifeline
http://www.suicidepreventionlifeline.org/
Number: 1-800-273-8255

Bullying
Bergin, D. & Cooks, H. 2002. "High school students of Color talk about accusations of 'acting white.' *The Urban Review* 34: 113-34.

Hochschild JL, Weaver V. "The Skin Color Paradox and the American Racial Order." Social Forces. 2007; 86(2):643-670.

Maddox, K. & Gray, S. 2002. "Cognitive Representations of Black Americans: Reexploring the Role of Skin Tone." PERSONALITY AND SOCIAL PSYCHOLOGY BULLETIN 28 (2): 250-59.

McArdle, C. & Young, N. 1970. "Classroom discussion of racial identity or how can we make it without 'acting white.' *American Journal of Orthopsychiatry* 41: 135-41.

Neal-Barnett, A. 2001. "Being black: New thoughts on the old phenomenon of acting white. Pp. 75-87 in

Forging Links: African American Children: Clinical Developmental Perspectives.

Pacer's National Bullying Prevention Center. (2015). Bullying info and facts. Retrieved from http://www.pacer.org/bullying/resources/info-facts.asp.

The Annual Bullying Survey. (2015). Key findings. Retrieved from http://www.ditchthelabel.org/annual-bullying-survey-2015/

The Diana Award Anti-Bullying Campaign (2015). Cyberbullying, bullying. Retrieved from http://www.antibullyingpro.com/blog/2015/4/7/facts-on-bullying

Movies

Darabont, F. (Producer) & Valdes, D. (Producer) & Darabont, F. (Director). (1999). *The Green Mile* [Motion Picture]. United States: Castle Rock Entertainment.

Finerman, W. (Producer), Starkey, S. (Producer), & Tisch, S. (Producer) & Zemeckis, R. (Director). (1994). *Forrest Gump* [Motion Picture]. United States: Paramount Pictures.

Zanuck, L.F. (Producer) & Zanuck, R.D. (Producer) & Beresford, B. (Director). (1989).*Driving Miss Daisy* [Motion Picture]. United States: The Zanuck Company.

Television Shows

Medina, B. (Writer), & Melman, J. (Director). (1990). Courting disaster. [Television series episode]. In A. Borowitz (Producer), *The Fresh Prince of Bel-Air*. Hollywood, CA: Hollywood Center Studios.

Winter, B. (Writer), & Jensen, S. (Director). (1992). That's no lady, that's my cousin! [Television series episode]. In J.Pollack (Producer), *The Fresh Prince of Bel-Air*. Brentwood, CA: NBC.

Yohe, T. (Producer). (1993). *Schoolhouse Rock!* [Television series]. American Broadcasting Company.

Yorkin, B. & Lear, N. (Producers). (1973). *Sanford and Son* [Television series]. Toluca, CA: NBC.

Poetry

Dunbar, P. (1896). We wear the mask.
Guest, E. (1937). It couldn't be done.
Hughes, L. (1951). Harlem.

Malloch, D. (1938). Be the best of whatever you are.

Shimon, L. (1936). I know something good about you. Wintle, W. (1905). Think.

Songs
Brown, C. (2011). Look at me now. On *F.A.M.E.* Los Angeles, Jive.

Brown, J. (1965). I feel good. On *Out of Sight*. Miami, King.

Speeches
Jackson, J. (1988, July). *1988 Democratic National Convention Address*. Speech presented at Omni Coliseum, Atlanta, GA.

King, M. (1963, August). *I Have a Dream*. Speech presented at the Lincoln Memorial, Washington, D.C.

Books
Dickens, C. (1859). *A tale of two cities*. London: Chapman & Hall.

Quotes
According to Vince Lombardi (1960), "the only place success comes before work is in the dictionary."

About the Author

Tensie J. Taylor is from Louisburg, North Carolina. She graduated from North Carolina State University in 2009 with a Bachelor of Arts in Communication—Media concentration—and a minor in Psychology and from the University of Southern California in 2014 with a Master of Education in Postsecondary Administration and Student Affairs. Currently, Tensie is the Assistant Director of the USC Black Alumni Association and in this role, she plans, coordinates, and executes programs and events for the Black Alumni Association; directs the Legacy through Leadership Mentorship Program, and assists with Toastmasters International. Tensie also serves on the Board of Directors for the We Are Ohana Foundation, an organization that is dedicated to finding resources and helping foster youth in Los Angeles.

In addition to working at USC, Tensie is a red carpet host for the online network *Rich Girl Network. TV*. As a host, she has interviewed numerous celebrities at galas, charity functions, community service events, award shows, and film festivals. Tensie has attended the Oscars, People's Choice

Awards, BET's Celebration of Gospel, NAACP Image Awards, Grammys, and BET Awards.

Tensie's hobbies include reading, writing, singing, playing the piano and trumpet, volunteering, mentoring young people, and traveling. One of Tensie's favorite quotes is by Mahatma Gandhi: *"Be the change that you wish to see in the world."*

Tensie has recited and traveled across the United States making presentations and speeches since the age of three. Tensie is available to speak at seminars, conferences, galas, awards shows, schools, colleges, universities, and churches. In addition, she is available to sing and play the piano and trumpet at celebrations, concerts, and performances. Tensie has played the piano nationally and internationally, including Europe and Africa.

This is Tensie's first published book.

Please submit all speaking and performance inquiries to: **ttaylorinquiries@gmail.com.**

Tensie J. Taylor's social media information is as follows:

Facebook Personal Page: Tensie Taylor
Facebook Fan Page: Tensie J. Taylor
Instagram: tensietaylor
Twitter: @MsTensie
YouTube: TensieT